EBURY PRESS
TEN YEARS WITH GURU DUTT

Sathya Saran is one of India's leading journalists and best known for her stint as editor of the popular women's magazine, *Femina*. Apart from short stories and a series of biographies on cinema and music greats, Saran has written extensively on issues concerning women. She has won a number of awards for her contribution to journalism. She lives in Mumbai with her family and dogs.

TEN YEARS *with*
GURU DUTT
ABRAR ALVI'S JOURNEY

SATHYA SARAN

EBURY
PRESS

An imprint of Penguin Random House

EBURY PRESS

USA | Canada | UK | Ireland | Australia
New Zealand | India | South Africa | China | Singapore

Ebury Press is part of the Penguin Random House group of companies
whose addresses can be found at global.penguinrandomhouse.com

Published by Penguin Random House India Pvt. Ltd
4th Floor, Capital Tower 1, MG Road,
Gurugram 122 002, Haryana, India

Penguin
Random House
India

First published in Viking by Penguin Books India 2008
Published in Penguin Books 2011
This edition published in Ebury Press by Penguin Random House India 2020

ISBN 9780143416920

Typeset in Gill Sans MT and Calisto MT by SÜRYA, New Delhi
Printed at Manipal Technologies Limited, India

www.penguin.co.in

MIX
Paper | Supporting
responsible forestry
FSC® C043100

To every filmgoer who has been enchanted by the magic of Guru Dutt's films

Contents

Introduction

The article I had just read got me thinking.

It was an interview with Abrar Alvi, in the *Indian Express*, and at the end of it, the writer threw out a challenge on behalf of the interviewee. Abrar Alvi had many stories to tell about his life and his work with Guru Dutt, if someone was willing to listen to them. Was there such a person around, the interviewer wondered.

Having always been fascinated by Indian cinema, the challenge intrigued me. I was at that time going through a rough patch emotionally, thanks to matters at the workplace turning sour. This, I told myself, would distract me, keep me from feeling that my journalistic job was the beginning and the end of the world.

I called Abrar and, referring to the article, offered my services. He was wary, yet interested. I proposed going over to meet him. He was not sure he wanted me to, but agreed half-heartedly. We were almost at the end of the conversation, when he asked me my name once more. I spelt it out to him.

'Saran?' he said. 'I thought Saral. I knew a Saran in Nagpur—'

'That must be my family,' I butted in.

It turned out, in the next ten minutes, that Abrar had known my husband's cousins closely. A warmth entered his voice; I could sense trust flooding in. And the date for our meeting was set.

It was the start of a long association of reminiscences and narrations. Every Saturday, I would take a train from V.T. Station (now Chhatrapati Shivaji Terminus) to Andheri, then a bus to his building and the lift up to his apartment on the tenth floor where, after I had taken off my footwear and was seated in a breezy corner of the drawing room by a window, Abrar would come in and we would start the process of recording, in my handwriting, the ten years of his life with one of India's most creative film-makers.

Surprisingly, my knowledge of Guru Dutt was not as deep as that of other directors, but as Abrar began narrating his stories I found myself living, vicariously, a life that was dominated by a mind that had many facets, many aspects of genius. Perhaps the fact that we share a date—he died on 10 October, the date (not the same year though) I was born—has something to do with it.

Abrar himself was fascinating. Equally fluent in Hindi, Urdu and English, he would reel out stories with amazing dexterity, sometimes meandering into a by-lane of thought, till I, patiently, deftly drew him back. He never took umbrage at the interruptions, having warned me himself that he was in the habit of losing the thread of his thoughts and that I should goad him back to the point from where he had wandered.

As the stories unfolded, sometimes chronologically, mostly at random, it dawned upon me that here was a very angry, bitter, disappointed man. His anger was directed at many things.

For one, he ranted about the fact that he was still being robbed of his right—the credit for directing Guru Dutt Films' most lauded, most awarded, film, *Sahib Bibi Aur Ghulam*. Critics have over the years insisted that Abrar was only a front for a director who had decided he did not want to take credit thanks to a superstition, resulting from the debacle of *Kaagaz Ke Phool*, that he was jinxed.

Abrar would bubble over when he came to that point. He had many ways of proving he was the man at the helm, that it was his baby from start to finish. He had proof, witnesses, and had produced them at times, but the doubt remained in people's minds—the suspicion, once planted, would not be erased. More than four decades after the film's release, it still hurt him that his finest hour was attributed to someone else.

It did not hurt him to live in the shadow of a great creative genius, though. As his tale unfolded, it was obvious that Abrar was the perfect foil, the reasonable mind, the method that kept the genius harnessed to reality and life. It did not hurt him to have his ideas scrapped, his contribution denied. In film after film, his credits did not appear. He wrote entire screenplays single-handedly and was credited only for the dialogues, but he was happy because he had found his métier. The angst hit him only when, after his directorial success, credit was not given to him by the world that would not accept an equal to Guru Dutt.

On many a Saturday, I spent the first hour of our meeting listening to him seething and fuming with frustration and despair: he would have watched a television interview in which someone he had worked with closely at Guru Dutt Films would mention everyone except him, and acknowledge his or her debt to all except him. He felt he did not exist, that the best years of his creative life had been erased, were being erased methodically and systematically by those who chose to ignore him, only because he was not a visible, powerful force any more.

It would take a lot of persuasion to calm him down, to get him back on track, make him understand that this book, when it came out, could undo some of the damage, could perhaps finally give him his place in the sun once again.

Yet it was not always a grim, challenging assignment. He could be funny, jovial, tell humorous stories with all the sound and action and mimicry of voices that a grandfather uses when telling stories to children—talents which he had used to advantage in the past, and which is one of the reasons *Sahib Bibi Aur Ghulam* turned out the way it did.

In fact, one of the highlights of my interaction with him was the tape he lent me, wherein he had recorded an Indian adaptation of the entire screenplay of *Fiddler on the Roof*. He had narrated the dialogues in all the characters' voices, making it so real that more than once I found myself on the verge of tears in the more poignant moments. The tape is still with him, and an enterprising director could make a hit if he chooses to, by getting Abrar Alvi to give him the rights to use the screenplay and dialogues.

A year and a bit after our Saturday trysts ended, and as the book is ready for release, Abrar Alvi is a very sick man. The many ailments that beset him—in his own words, 'Any ailment you name, I have it'—keep him confined to his bed. His meandering mind tends to drift all the more easily, though when I call him on the phone to ask him questions that the book's wonderful editor, Shantanu, asks, he is clear in his replies.

I do wish he finds happiness again and the book vindicates his stand and places him firmly back in public memory; that future generations, who thrill to the world-class cinema Guru Dutt Films produced, will know him as the man who was friend, philosopher and guide to Guru Dutt, and the writer and director of *Sahib Bibi Aur Ghulam*.

1

Bichde Sabhi Bari Bari

In the last scene of *Baharen Phir Bhi Aayengi* (1966), the heroine dies. A sad, lonely, disappointed death. Disillusioned by life, forsaken by those she loves, she suffers a heart attack. Writing such a scene is not easy. Especially if one has not experienced death at close quarters. It needs empathy, concentration and sensitivity to invest the scene with enough to bring it to life.

The date was 9 October 1964. In the drawing room of Ark Royal, Guru Dutt's flat on Peddar Road, Abrar Alvi, Guru Dutt's friend and working partner in all his films for the past ten years, sat working on the scene, his task made doubly difficult by the mood that seemed to have settled over the evening. And over Guru Dutt himself.

I came to Ark Royal at about seven that evening and realized that Guru Dutt had been drinking. He had imbibed quite a lot already. For the past few days it had been my practice to spend the day at a flat nearby on Napean Sea Road working on a script for a film by Lekh Tandon. But every evening, I would come over to Ark

Royal—that was the condition under which I had been released to write the film. Guru Dutt would come back to his flat only in the evenings, after spending the day at Natraj Studios. And we would spend the evening companionably together, talking, discussing work.

But this evening his mood seemed particularly sombre. I was not sure how long he had been drinking. I asked his Man Friday, Ratan, what his day had been like, and Ratan replied, 'He has been drinking since five-thirty this evening.' I tried to lighten his mood. 'What's the grieving about . . . where's the cause for sorrow?' I asked, but Guru Dutt was non-committal. He just smiled his half-smile and poured himself another drink.

I settled down to write my scene. A mutual friend, Gole, an income-tax officer, dropped in. We chatted of this and that, and Gole joined Guru Dutt in drinking. I continued to grapple with the scene on hand. The two of them, Guru Dutt and Gole, would float away downstairs to a distributor's flat to talk on the phone. But naturally, while they were there, they would down a few drinks to keep the distributor company. Then they would come up, and sit around chatting, drinking.

I told them to eat, it was getting late; I would eat later after the scene was finished. But Guru Dutt would not have that. 'I'll wait for you,' he said, and wandered off to make another phone call.

His mood worsened. He had had a tiff of some kind with Geeta (his estranged wife). She had refused to send across their baby daughter so that he could spend time with her, and with each call his anger mounted. At last, he had delivered an ultimatum . . . or so he seemed to suggest. 'Send the child or you will see my dead body . . .' You know, the kind of things one says when one is angry and one's tongue gets a bit out of control.

Then, he started to muse about a call he had made to Raj Kapoor. 'Maybe I should not have asked him to come across . . . I must be high . . . I don't know him well enough to call him so casually, he might misinterpret it . . .'

Gole broke into his reverie. 'I have to go to work tomorrow, let's eat,' he said. Gole lived in Bandra and worked in town and he would have to go back home and return all the way the next day. But Guru Dutt wanted to wait for me to finish. Finally Gole was persuaded to eat alone, after which he left.

I finished the scene close to midnight and we prepared to eat. Guru Dutt wanted to have one more drink before dinner, and so by the time we ate, it was almost one a.m. He had downed quite a bit by then, but neither of us was in the habit of losing control of our senses. We would get a bit unsteady—that was all. However, when we finally got down to eating, he merely nibbled at the food. I was hungry by then and polished off a decent meal.

Throughout the meal he was monosyllabic. And then, brushing aside my attempts at conversation, he said, 'If you don't mind, I would like to retire.'

I asked him, 'What of the scene I have written?' It was his habit to listen to a scene once it was done, but he would have none of it. He told me to leave it with Ratan and went to his room.

For many months now my room had been across his, on the other side of the corridor. But that night I left as I had to work on Lekh's film in the morning. I gave the scene to Ratan and told him not to let Guru Dutt drink any more. 'I am going to Lekh Tandon's house on Napean Sea Road,' I added, before leaving. I never saw Guru Dutt alive again.

Few people know the sequence of events after Abrar Alvi left Ark Royal on the fateful night that was to be the last night in the life of one of India's most iconoclastic film-makers. Guru Dutt, whose work lives after him and continues to inspire generations of film-makers and students of cinema, spent his last night in a manner as dramatic as any scene from one of his own films. Abrar Alvi learnt of the last hours of his life from Ratan, only when it was already too late.

❧

It must have been about three a.m. when Guru Dutt woke up and came out of his room. He woke Ratan and demanded to know where I was. He had walked across to my room and seen it empty. Ratan told him that I had left after giving him the scene I had written. 'Should I call him?' Ratan asked.

It was not unusual for me to be woken from deep sleep and called to Guru Dutt's side—in the past I had been whisked to his home to discuss an idea, to watch chickens hatching in his incubator, or to share his thoughts—and Ratan would have called me, but Guru Dutt thought for a moment and shook his head. 'Let it be,' he said, and asked for a bottle of whisky.

Ratan told him the whisky was finished.

But Guru Dutt was not to be appeased. He knew there had to be a bottle or two stashed away; the guy who got us the booze brought in half a dozen bottles at a time. So he looked around and finally found a bottle. Holding it in one hand, he went back to his room. Ratan heard him lock the door from inside.

The next morning, Geeta Dutt called. She wanted to know if sahib was awake.

❧

In a report in *Filmfare* a month after Guru Dutt's death, Nargis went on record saying that Geeta was restless through the night with a strange premonition. She had wanted to visit Guru Dutt that night at about eleven, but her mother was uneasy about her going out alone so late and had dissuaded her.

Geeta woke again at about two a.m., full of dread, though there was no apparent reason. And thus it was that at eight-thirty in the morning she called, wanting to talk to Guru Dutt. Ratan told her that his master had retired very late and was therefore still asleep.

Filmfare reports too that Guru Dutt's personal physician also dropped in at about nine a.m. But he left without seeing Guru Dutt, because he was still behind the locked door of his room.

Geeta called every half hour, and just before eleven a.m., told Ratan to break open the door.

The door was broken down. Guru Dutt lay in his bed, apparently in deep sleep. The physician returned at eleven and declared him dead. He had been dead for some time.

I do believe that there was something ominous in the fact that Geeta asked Ratan to break the door. It must have been because of the conversation they had, and his words of anger; they must have rankled and made her suspect something was not quite right. Otherwise, it is quite normal for a man who has drunk so heavily, so long into the night, to sleep it off at least till noon.

However, I knew nothing of the drama taking place at Ark Royal. At about noon, Lekh told me to go across to Guru Dutt's house as he had been taken ill.

I told myself he must have pulled one of his stunts, taken a tablet to worry us, to trouble all of us.

I went across to Ark Royal. Guru Dutt lay on his bed in his kurta pyjama. On the bedside table was a glass with a little pink liquid still left in it.

'He's killed himself!' I exclaimed.

They asked me how I knew. Of course I knew; we had discussed it so many times.

'It's Sonaril,' I told them. He used to get it through his driver from a chemist in Khar. I had even scolded the pharmacist and threatened to report him for selling drugs without a proper prescription. We used to talk about it: the ways to kill oneself. I had even tried it once, and he had at least twice before. And we had realized that a man cannot kill himself by swallowing sleeping pills. By the time you can swallow a lethal dose, the medicine overpowers you and you conk out.

He had worked it out. He told me, 'You must take it like a mother gives medicine to her child . . . crush the tablets and dissolve them in water.'

At that time we were actually mocking the idea of suicide. If only I had known that he would put the jest to the test . . .

∽

Thus, on 10 October 1964, with this scene that Abrar had not written, ended a chapter in his life—a chapter that had spanned ten long, eventful, tumultuous years, years of a close and unforgettable association with Guru Dutt. Abrar Alvi's life would never be the same again.

2

Baat Kuch Ban Hi Gayi

The story began in 1953, when Guru Dutt was still a star whose light was yet to shine. The film he was shooting for was *Baaz*, being made under the banner of Haridarshan Gurudutt Films. Guru Dutt was a partner in the company with Haridarshan Kaur (fondly called Bibiji), who was Geeta Bali's sister. He was directing the film and also playing the role of the hero. The heroine? Geeta Bali, of course.

Cast in the role of second or 'side hero', as the terminology went those days, was a young, handsome charmer called Yashwant. His role in the film was to romance Geeta Bali's friend, Yashodra Katju. Off-screen, Yashwant was in the process of charming the producer herself, who in turn was quite taken by his gallant ways and good looks, and laboured under the delusion that her beau, though footloose and fancy-free, would take her for his wife. Yashwant was Abrar's cousin.

It was thanks to Yashwant that Abrar got a foothold in the film industry. He had worked as assistant director to C.L. Dheer in *Bahu Beti*, starring, among others, Yashwant. Dheer, seeing Abrar's astute understanding of emotions and histrionics, had taken him on to work with his actors on the sets before each scene. And Abrar, while looking for the means to fund his own digs, lived with

Yashwant and his rather large extended family.

Playing the role of minor star to the hilt, Yashwant had bought himself a car, a Hillman, which he wanted to drive to the sets of *Baaz*. There was only one problem. Yashwant had never learnt to drive.

That was when Abrar was asked to repay the debt he owed his cousin. He would drive Yashwant to the sets every day. Anyway he had nothing else on hand, and the exposure would do him good. It did not take long for Abrar to graduate from driver to chaperone. When *Baaz*'s comely producer, Haridarshan Kaur, wanted to go shopping she turned to the man who had two very good qualifications: he could drive, and he was the cousin of the man who was courting her and could guide her on what she could buy for him.

The shopping trips and his proximity to the producer helped draw Abrar into the inner circle. And soon 'Lord Falkland', as the unit quickly nicknamed him, was lunching with the heroine, the producer and, of course, the hero, Guru Dutt.

Being on the sets had its advantages. Abrar found himself a friend in Guru Dutt's chief assistant, Raj Khosla. As the friendship developed, Raj Khosla came to know that Abrar held a postgraduate degree, had a law degree and a more than nodding experience in many aspects of theatre and radio thanks to his active role in both during his college days. It brought him in direct touch with the man who was to be his mentor, friend and confidant for a whole decade. Abrar's first impressions of Guru Dutt are worth recounting.

∽

Guru Dutt was a man of few words. My only interaction with him those days was to say 'good morning' and 'goodnight'. He was not a very communicative person, and I had no reason to approach him or start a conversation with him. But very early on I realized that he had a habit of changing a scene even when he was in the process of shooting it. He was the sort of director who was never happy with his writers. One day, after lunch, I was sitting around in the improvised recording room which had a cane sofa set and a tarpaulin top. Raj Khosla came in holding a pen and a sheet of paper. He was trying to rewrite a scene in a particular way, incorporating the changes that Guru Dutt wanted. I let him work, and continued to sit there, trying not to let my presence disturb him. Soon Guru Dutt joined him, and sat waiting to hear the scene.

Suddenly Raj turned to me, to ask my opinion. He read out a sentence. He of course expected me to say 'wah wah', as is the wont of hangers-on at film studios. However, my critical sensibilities were not to be denied. I told him that the sentence was fine grammatically, but it was not so easy for me to give him an opinion of its real quality. 'Unless I know the characters, the background, I cannot say if the dialogue fits,' I added.

And in his own characteristic way, Abrar Alvi went on to give Raj Khosla an impromptu treatise on dialogue writing and characterization. Raj Khosla listened, maybe with some impatience. There was work to be done, a scene to be delivered and the director was waiting. 'He insisted the line fitted the scene perfectly,' Abrar says, 'and I let him go ahead. I dropped the matter.'

He did not know it then, but Guru Dutt had been paying close attention to Abrar's speech to Raj Khosla. Two or three days later, he asked Yashwant about his cousin. According to Abrar, 'When he heard that I was an MA, LLB, he told Yashwant, "Send him to me quickly."'

But Yashwant could not oblige. Abrar was nowhere to be found.

A doctor friend of Abrar's had consulted an astrologer, who, in the way astrologers have, held out a bunch of vague hopes. As he gazed into Abrar's future, he intoned, 'By end June, something significant will happen.'

Abrar's birthday falls on 1 July. He expected a few gifts, that's all. There was, despite his friend's constant reminder through the rest of the day, no reason to believe that a windfall of any sort was coming his way.

Quite enjoying being his own master, Abrar had been leading a double life. One saw him at the studios, as an extension of his cousin. The other saw him trailing his college persona behind him, where he cohabited with friends from his past.

It was in one such mood that he had taken himself away from the claustrophobia of the sets of *Baaz*, where he had no real role to play beyond odd man watching, to visit his friend Tully.

A doctor with the KEM Hospital in Parel, Tully had been one of his first saviours in the big, bad city of Bombay. He had shared his hostel room with the homeless, penniless Abrar, till they had got found out and Abrar was forced to look for alternative accommodation. However, Abrar was still a familiar face, and the watchmen were quite open to being bribed into silence. And Abrar would, whenever he needed a break, willingly part with the few rupees that would get him into the medical college hostel and enable him to share Tully's room again.

Two or three days of inaction were enough, and Abrar would wind his way back to Juhu, to enter the overfull home he shared with his cousin's family.

I was quite unprepared for the wrath that awaited me when I went back this time. There was no sign of the promised windfall. Instead,

Yashwant paced the floor, foaming at the mouth. 'How can you go away without informing me, where do you go . . .'

When he had calmed down, I asked him what the matter was.

'He's been asking about you, he has sent his car for you twice already . . . I had nothing to say to him that made sense . . . I just did not know where you were . . .'

Stemming another impending tirade, I managed to ask who it was who had been so anxious to meet me.

'Why! Guru Dutt, of course,' he responded.

'Why would he want to meet me?' I countered. '*Baaz* is being wrapped up, and there will be a huge gap before the next round of casting begins for another venture . . .'

I had often pestered Raj Khosla to get me a bit role, so I could stand on my own feet, but this was much too early.

'I don't know, and I don't care,' Yashwant rumbled. 'You will go to meet Guru Dutt. And you will go now. Now!'

With that he propelled me to the door and let me out.

I was so broke that I could not hurry. I knew there were no direct buses . . . I hung around till a bus came and took the long, hot road to Guru Dutt's house on 7th Road, Khar.

3

Aaj Mujhe Neend
Nahin Aayegi

Abrar had gone to meet Guru Dutt as per his cousin's instructions. Anyone who has waited for an audience with a film celebrity— whether he is hero, director or producer—knows the agony of it. Even when the star has given an appointment, there is no guarantee that it will be honoured. Even if it is, chances are that one will have to wait till one's patience has worn thin. Guru Dutt was producer, director and hero rolled into one. So Abrar Alvi waited, expecting to do so a very long time. Surprisingly, Guru Dutt materialized rather quickly. And even before Abrar Alvi could put his thoughts in place for an introduction, Guru Dutt shocked him by asking if Abrar was willing to write for Guru Dutt Films.

∾

I was floored. I was afraid that I would fall short of expectations. I told him, 'I am not a writer . . . I have only written a few stage plays and that sort of thing.' But he seemed to have made up his mind. He said, 'I have a strong feeling that you will make a very good writer

... your cousin says you are educated, and anyway, I heard you when you gave Khosla that talk.'

I was still diffident. He was after all an established producer and hero. I offered him my plays ... he could read them and assess whether I had what he wanted in his writer, but he turned me down. 'No,' he said, 'come tomorrow and I will give you a situation. You develop it and I will listen to the scene. If I like it, you work for me, if I don't ... well I'll tell you so.'

The meeting was over. Abrar went away wondering what was in store for him. A brand-new career seemed to be opening up and on the way back he had visions of being financially independent at long last. He was making Rs 150 a month as assistant director, and it just about covered his expenses. He could barely wait for the night to end. Guru Dutt had asked him to come to his residence at nine a.m. the next day. Abrar was there at eight-thirty. Guru Dutt met him on time and invited him to breakfast.

I was not in the habit of breakfast. My resources did not allow me the luxury of eating three times a day, so I declined. Guru Dutt gave me the situation and told me to write a scene. He spent a little time asking me a few details on how I would develop the character. I, in turn, asked him a few questions on the character, and then he said, 'I am going to my office.' I told him I would bring the scene to him when I was done with it and got up to leave. But he said, 'No, sit here and write. I might drop in by twelve-thirty or so to see how it is progressing.'

He called his cook, and pointing to me said, 'Make sure he is comfortable, give him food when he gets hungry, give him tea whenever he needs it.' I did not realize it then, but I was a virtual hostage in his house. I finished writing the scene by three-thirty, but there was no sign of the man. I was told he would come any minute, so I waited. I had to read the scene to him. He finally returned at five-thirty. I read out the scene to him. He listened with gravity and deep interest.

I looked at him expectantly . . . was it what he expected?

He looked back at me, then said, 'Hmmm.'

I stared at him.

He said, 'Come again tomorrow.'

'What do you think of the scene?'

'Come tomorrow, we shall discuss it then.'

I had no choice but to leave the scene behind.

∽

Like scenes from a suspense film, the next few days went by in a haze. Day after day, a situation was narrated and then Abrar was virtually isolated from all human contact while he wrote the scene. For seven whole days, the performance was repeated. Abrar wished desperately to know the outcome of this peculiar 'test' that he was being put to. While he waited, Abrar went over the possibilities.

∼

After a couple of days I think I began to understand the reason for this strange mode of writing that I was being subjected to: he did not want me to consult anybody. He was not taking any chances. I adapted to the situation. I wrote, ate, slept for a while in the afternoons, got up and completed the scene, and waited for the man to come and see it. He would listen and make no comment, and I knew I would be back the next day.

I wanted to meet Raj Khosla. He would be able to throw some light on Guru Dutt's strange behaviour, I thought. But Raj was in Dalhousie, mooning over Nutan. Raj was, in those days, a character straight out of P.G. Wodehouse. In and out of love, and each time it was for real. The man went to Dalhousie for two days, to set things up for a shoot, fell in love with Nutan and hung around for all of fifteen days. Meanwhile, I was going through the most suspenseful days of my life.

Then it happened. I had finished the scene as usual and wanted to read it out to Guru Dutt. But he asked me to wait. 'I have to freshen up,' he explained. 'I have a meeting with Rajinder Singh Bedi and Majrooh Sultanpuri.'

I was disheartened. As he left the room I told myself, This is the end. If he was going to call Majrooh and Bedi, why put me through this test? I knew I must have failed him. But he had asked me to wait . . . perhaps he would make me assist Bedi . . .

I knew Bedi quite well. I had worked with him on C.L. Dheer's *Bahu Beti*. I had rehearsed the actors through the film, and knew the dialogues Bedi had written almost by heart. I knew Majrooh quite well too, and of his close connection with Bedi.

When Majrooh saw me, he asked what I was doing there. I told him. He said rather magnanimously, 'I'll tell him that you are a good assistant director, that you are educated.'

Then Guru Dutt came in and called them into the inner room. I sat alone while they talked. They left a little later and Guru Dutt came over to me. I picked up my papers and said, '*Scene sunaun*?'

He said, '*Rehne do*.' He was deep in thought, a bit distracted.

I was quite despondent by now. I said, 'Can I go?'

He flared up. '*Kya ratt laga rakhi hai*!' he exclaimed. 'You can't go, we need to talk.'

So I sat down. He asked me my opinion of Bedi. As was

expected of me, I began singing his praise. 'He is hundred per cent, he is the best, I am but a 10 in comparison,' I said, knowing that I needed to give him an excuse to turn me down. 'He is incomparable,' I continued.

Guru Dutt started laughing. 'Why are you comparing him then?' he asked, and continued to laugh.

I said, 'Yes, I know he is so good, I should not even compare myself with him.'

He nodded. Then, even as I prepared to leave while I still had my dignity intact, he said, 'I have met Bedi and listened to him because Majrooh insisted I should do so. But now I am convinced that you will write for me. Bedi says directors don't even bring ten per cent of what he writes to life. He might say that of me as well if I direct what he writes. I have heard you for seven days. I want you to write my next film.'

❧

Abrar is, for a change, at a loss for words as he relives this moment. But his face reflects the joy he must have felt then, the sheer pleasure of being accepted on merit. Needless to say, he said yes immediately. Then Guru Dutt added his rider. Abrar would write for him on one condition: he would have to be present on the sets all the time, and help direct the actors in emoting and in delivering their lines. Abrar readily agreed. The rest of his life had begun.

Abrar Alvi did not know it then, but there were two other people, besides Guru Dutt, who were watching his progress rather closely.

❧

I often spoke to Sharashar Sailani, one of the many writers working on *Baaz*. One day I narrated to him two scenes I had written. He had become quite a friend, so I could trust him to give me an honest opinion. He listened intently, then sat silently for a long time, his head bowed.

I grew anxious. 'What is it?' I asked, a bit testily.

Sailani looked up at me and said, 'You have passed the test, *aap ne imtehan pass kar liya hai*, Dutt cannot fail you now.'

∽

Abrar also learnt later that besides this recommendation from a rival writer, the final okay came from no less than the actor–director's mother. She was a bilingual writer, who wrote in Kannada and Bengali, and Guru Dutt held her opinion in great esteem. It was much later that Abrar came to know that she had read Abrar's scenes and told her son that she liked the tone and flow of the writing. That must have influenced Guru Dutt, and Abrar believes she was one of the reasons he was signed on as writer for Guru Dutt Films.

4

Kaliyan Ki Muskaan Hai

If it hadn't been for the 300 love letters he had written, Abrar Alvi could not have probably risen to the challenge Guru Dutt had posed before him.

The story goes back to his college days. Abrar had managed to convince his father that he was not cut out for science. It had taken all of one wasted academic year but at the end of it, Abrar was allowed to shift to an arts college.

Hislop College in Nagpur was a venerable institution of learning in those days. But I was not a star student. Being the son of an IPS officer who believed in body building, I ended up with enough muscles to take pride in my physique and was convinced of my superior physical strength.

I went through the first year of my BA course flexing my muscles and bullying my classmates. I built up an unflattering reputation of being a nasty fellow who ridiculed others and had a strong malicious streak. Of course, it was my immaturity which made me behave the way I did, but luckily for me, I soon got wise.

Knowing that my reputation would do me no good academically, I changed colleges. I took a transfer to Morris College, and turned over a new leaf.

~

Abrar's competitive spirit took a new form. He participated in debates and elocutions and, more often than not, walked away with a clutch of prizes in both the English and Hindi categories. By the end of his first year in Morris College, he had found himself a mentor in Professor Dharmaraj who headed the YMCA where Abrar had taken a room. 'I discovered my potential under his guidance,' he says. 'I soon became a fine orator and began to take part in plays.'

Before long he was writing and directing plays not just for his own college but for the annual day functions of five colleges, and was recognized as the best freelance dramatist. He earned a reputation as a confident director who could entice performances from even utter novices. He did not know it then, but it was a skill that Guru Dutt would exploit to the advantage of Indian cinema.

Abrar could wring out a credible performance from males playing female roles in college plays, but he did dream of the day he would be able to direct women.

~

The opportunity came when I was in my MA previous year. Nagpur Medical College approached me to direct a play for their annual day, and I agreed on the condition that I would be allowed to cast actresses for the female roles.

Of course there were no women ready to take up the parts, but I was confident that I could persuade anyone. I told the students' union, 'Show me someone with potential and I will do the rest.' They pointed out a young medical student from Lucknow. She was a Christian, and that made me believe she would be more open-minded to taking to the stage. I was, however, told that she had been sounded out and had proved unwilling.

I scouted around, finding out more about her. She lived in the YWCA, which meant there were no parents to contend with. That, I told my friends, will make my task easier. I decided to try and convince her to take on a role in my play. If she agreed, I knew it would start a trend and break the unspoken taboo about women getting on to the stage.

One fine evening, I went across to meet her at the YWCA. She came up to me, looked me in the eye, and said with uncommon frankness, 'So you are Abrar Alvi.' I was struck by her open gaze, her frank manner. There was none of the coy bashfulness that marked the behaviour of most college girls of that time especially in their interactions with boys.

I set about talking her into acting. After much argument, she agreed to write to her father and ask him for his views on the matter. Of course, her father said no, he wanted her to concentrate on her medical studies. The evening she told me about her father's decision, we talked till it turned dark. I remonstrated with her, hoping to change her mind. Also, somewhere along the way, I had begun to realize that she was attracted to me, and that was reason enough for me to spend time with her.

But she would not cross her father's will. I got up to leave. She walked to the gate with me. Seeing that it had become quite dark, she took off the lamp from her bicycle and hooked it on to my lampless one. 'I won't be able to forgive myself if you get caught without a light,' she said by way of explanation. 'You can return the lamp tomorrow.'

The cycle lamp became an excuse for us to meet every evening. The play went into rehearsal without her. We persuaded another young girl to take on the challenge of the role, but I continued to visit the YWCA regularly. Almost every evening, come five-thirty, I would meet her at her hostel, we would talk till it was dark, and at seven-thirty, I would ride away bearing her cycle light on my bicycle.

Then one day, I lost my temper over something she said and scolded her. I raised my voice and saw her eyes fill with sudden tears. I left, angry and confused. That night, I wrote her a letter. It was my first letter, and it reflected all the thoughts that I had not spoken, all the confusion of my feelings for her.

I was worried after I sent her the letter. What would she think, what would her reaction be? Had I gone too far in expressing myself? But, the curiosity of the writer to check out his audience overcame my trepidation. After many hours of indecision I went across to see her.

She greeted me with a smile. 'I received a beautiful letter today,' she said. 'I wish I could get such letters every day.'

I was elated. 'You will,' I said grandly. And I kept the promise. I did not realize then, but it was my first brush with the discipline of daily writing, and of pushing my creativity to perform on command.

The vacations made it easy for me to keep my word. She went back to Lucknow, I went home to Bhopal, and the letters were our link through the months. In each letter I would address her differently. I never ever used her name, and I would ensure that each letter was as fresh and as engrossing as the previous one.

I started sending her a fair copy, neatly written, and I would keep the fevered original with me. In the evenings when my friends gathered, I would read out my letters to them and ask their opinion on a turn of phrase or an expression of emotion. Soon my friends began to call me the specialist . . . they would approach me to write their love letters, or solve their love problems . . .

∽

The writer in Abrar Alvi had found his voice. He became aware of his metamorphosis into a performing artist, a writer who writes for applause. And he knew in his subconscious mind that this was the first step towards his true vocation. Abrar Alvi's final vindication of his writing skills came from an unusual source: union leader A.B. Bardhan, who, hiding from the authorities at the time, along with another union leader M.K. Vyas, came to seek shelter for a night and went on to share Abrar's room for six months.

❧

I was living in a chawl as the YMCA did not allow postgraduate students to rent rooms. A railway strike was imminent, and the union leader A.B. Bardhan had to go underground. Bardhan and I had worked together in the college union. He had been president of the union while I had been an active member. Thus, when he approached me, asking if he and M.K. Vyas could stay for a night in my room, I did not refuse.

They had plenty of time in hand, especially during the long days when I went to college. They read everything they could lay their hands on, including my letters. Bardhan told me one evening, 'Your letters are literary pieces. You should publish them.' That was when I was finally convinced I could write.

I created a file of my letters, and when my friends asked me for help to write a letter, I would tell them to look through the file, choose the one that worked best for them and copy it out.

❧

Bardhan's encouragement spurred Abrar Alvi. His professional life as a writer, which had started with playwriting, had taken its first definite step.

5

Kabhi Aar Kabhi Paar

The review section of *Filmfare* dated 7 August 1953 had this to say about *Baaz*:

> What could have been a good swashbuckling adventure film is here reduced to a comparatively tame picture owing to the inadequate direction and unknowing treatment of an otherwise action-packed story ... The drawing of the Portuguese characters in the film is naively done and shows a conspicuous lack of polish, especially in the direction ...

The review goes on to trash almost everything in the film and ends with a damning indictment of Guru Dutt the actor: 'Dutt as the hero is not dashing enough, and plays the part too tamely ...'

'I thought it was a mad idea, even at that time,' Abrar Alvi says of *Baaz*. 'It was a crazy drama on the high seas, with Geeta Bali as a lady pirate, and shots of sailboats tossing in the waters as pirates engaged in swordfights. With the technology available those days, it was a completely impractical story and setting, but the producers had been talked into it, and went along gamely. I told Guru Dutt this picture would not run, and we had a few discussions on it ...'

Discussions would be the leitmotif of the initial relationship between Abrar Alvi and his producer–director–actor boss, Guru Dutt.

By the time Abrar began writing for Guru Dutt, *Aar Paar* was already under way. As always, work on the script of the film went on even as shooting schedules continued to roll. That was the way most of Guru Dutt's films were shot, with one exception: *Sahib Bibi Aur Ghulam*. There was a definite reason for the exception, but that is another story, to be told later. For now, Abrar goes on to talk about his early days as assistant-on-the-sets and writer with the Guru Dutt Films unit.

∼

Nabendu Ghosh and Guru Dutt were working on the scenes of *Aar Paar*. A number of scenes had been done; I had been given only a few scenes to write. But by the time the film was one-third of the way through, I was the only person on the sets who was influencing Guru Dutt.

Of course, my friend and Guru Dutt's assistant, Raj Khosla, was there too, but if there was an unspoken, implied tussle between me and Raj as to who would wield the greater influence on Guru Dutt, I ultimately won. Perhaps it was because I always thought logically, always reasoned things out, and if anyone could prove me wrong after I had explained my reasoning, I would accept it. Guru Dutt respected that. He accepted it.

By the time *Aar Paar* was a little over one-third complete, the die had been cast. Ghosh was seldom around, and Raj Khosla was, almost as a face-saving tactic, allowed to take on another film. Guru Dutt and I carried on with the story and screenplay, taking the film forward. Slowly, very cautiously but surely, I turned the story of *Aar Paar* towards an emotional climax.

Guru Dutt approved of it. And the climax was shot. The scene required a consummate artist, which Guru Dutt was not. At least not at that time. His voice, his histrionic abilities had still to develop. Even his mannerisms were still quite raw. But the scene was canned.

Then Guru Dutt, with one of his lightning changes of mood, decided to shoot the climax once again. Differently. He decided on an action climax, fights, chase scene and all. We went through an eighteen-day re-shooting schedule, which was a lot, considering the entire movie had taken only seventy days to complete.

I had to hold my peace over the climax. Guru Dutt was in no mood to listen to my opinion of it. Not that he was a yes-man the rest of the time. The sets of *Aar Paar* witnessed really stormy scenes. We would have such heated verbal battles that people on the sets would think that I would hit him, or vice-versa. Very often, Raj Khosla would be instrumental in setting us off. Sometimes it would be Johnny Walker. They would take sides in an ongoing argument between us, provoking us further. At times, when I had decided on a certain approach to a scene and had managed to convince Guru Dutt about the same, a sly hint from Raj would get Guru Dutt thinking on another track, leading to arguments.

Guru Dutt seemed happy with the new version of the climax, and decided to keep it and scrap the earlier, emotional one. It was only later that Abrar Alvi came to know the real reason for Guru Dutt's change of mind. As Abrar found out, the idea for the new climax did not originate from Guru Dutt himself. 'K.K. Kapoor was at the root of it,' Abrar explains.

K.K. Kapoor was the producer of *Aar Paar* and had a three-film contract with Guru Dutt Films. With his characteristic recklessness, Guru Dutt had carved out his enterprise after the debacle of *Baaz* by buying over Haridarshan Kaur's share. And K.K. Kapoor had come in providentially with the finances to keep the director afloat. That he was financing the film gave Kapoor enough clout to dictate its climax.

6

Apne Pe Bharosa Hai Toh Yeh Daav Laga Le

Aar Paar has a special significance in the evolution of Guru Dutt Films. It blazed a trail that sooner or later the entire film industry would follow. It was also the beginning of the collaboration between Guru Dutt and Abrar Alvi. A collaboration that would find each fuelling the other's creativity and imagination, resulting in celluloid creations that have stood the test of time and are considered unparalleled classics of Indian cinema. Hired by Guru Dutt as dialogue writer, among his other roles, for *Aar Paar*, Abrar had his chance to realize a long-standing dream. But there was a rub.

∽

I think my first contribution to Guru Dutt Films was to change the way dialogues were being written. Even in my college days, while watching a film I used to find myself getting quite irritated with the way the dialogues had been penned. I found them artificial and stilted. It was of course a legacy of the theatre, but the fact remained that the speech was nothing close to the way the common man spoke. I used to think to myself then, 'If ever I get a chance to write for films, I will write the dialogues in the language of the character.'

With *Aar Paar*, I got my chance. But there was a problem. Raj Khosla believed that the language of cinema should be chaste. He had reason to think that way. His education had been in Urdu through his school, and even in college he had Urdu as one of his subjects. His reading of the Urdu greats had made a purist out of him.

In *Baaz*, the technique of dialogue writing went somewhat like this: the writer would write the first line of the dialogue and ask his assistant to speak it out while he searched his mind for a second line that would rhyme with and continue the first line. Sometimes the assistant would speak the line up to forty times before the dialogue writer could find a second line that could take the first forward with a rhyme or at least with a line that had a poetic flow to it.

Naturally, such dialogue writing was forced and the dialogues had an affected, unnatural quality to them.

❧

Raj Khosla had also influenced Guru Dutt into believing that Guru Dutt knew very little Hindi. It was not difficult to do that. Compared to Khosla, Guru Dutt had had little exposure to Hindi. He had grown up in Calcutta, and could speak Bengali fluently, and perhaps read and write it to some extent too. His mother tongue was Konkani. Hindi was at best a third language for him. Little wonder he let Raj Khosla, with his literary background in Urdu and Hindustani, show him the way, at least where dialogues were concerned. Abrar set about changing the equation.

❧

The first thing I did was to get Guru Dutt to believe in himself. I told him that there was no need to be lettered in a language to be able to handle dialogues realistically. I myself had had an English-medium education, but I could manage quite well in Hindi and Urdu. Surely, I impressed upon him, his Hindi was as good as mine. I also told Guru Dutt and his team that the best way to write dialogues for films so that they would be remembered was to break away from the theatre tradition. I told him, you have to write wrong to write right.

When Guru Dutt and Raj Khosla looked perplexed at his statement, Abrar added that knowing a language well enough to write in it also meant that one knew it well enough to break the syntax in such a way that it sounded as close to the spoken word as possible. And the permutations that people used while speaking were endless.

Abrar's views would be like a glove thrown into the ring and more often than not Raj Khosla would pick up the gauntlet. Guru Dutt would, in the beginning, find himself torn between his two assistants: one tried and trusted, the other new, but full of his own ideas, and tempting Guru Dutt to experiment boldly.

Sometimes Guru Dutt would argue with me over a point. He would say, 'But Raj Khosla says . . .' I would at some point lose my cool and say, '*Usi se karva lo aap* (get him to do it then).'

The skirmishes between us were many. Actually both of us were deeply engrossed in our work, and would end up starting an argument on how something should be done, and without even realizing it, would argue loud and long enough to have the entire unit stop their work and watch.

Johnny Walker used to say to me, 'There were times we thought either you would catch him by the throat or he would grab you and shake you.' But we would get over the argument soon enough and move on after one of us saw the other's point of view. That way there was absolutely no rancour on the sets. In fact, Guru Dutt used to admire me for holding on to my point of view unless I was convinced otherwise. That I had strong views and the conviction to hold on to them and argue them out evoked Guru Dutt's respect.

M.A. Latif, who had written the dialogues for Guru Dutt's *Jaal*, told me this later. I was working on *Aar Paar* and everyone on the sets knew that I had no experience of writing dialogues for films. Nor was I a published writer. One day, it seems, Kuldip Kahir, another writer who had worked with Guru Dutt, approached him along with Latif and said, 'Why don't you let us also collaborate, we have worked with you in earlier films, and Abrar is after all a new hand.' Guru Dutt reportedly told the two writers that he was more than satisfied with his new writer, his words being, 'He is enough for me, I do not want anyone else. He has a mind of his own . . . he is not a yes-man.'

I did get a reputation of being a fighter. Guru Dutt's brother Atma Ram once told me, 'You cannot work with anybody.' I told him, 'I cannot tolerate anyone talking like an idiot.' The prerequisite of any discussion is that you must be open to being convinced. If you are not convinced, you must convince. Having a closed mind is not going to help anybody, it will solve nothing.

∼

Abrar convinced Guru Dutt about his approach to dialogue writing. By the time one-third of *Aar Paar* was shot, Raj Khosla had left the film. The producer of *Jaal* had offered Khosla a film with Dev Anand and Geeta Bali, and he jumped at the chance of rising to the status of a full-fledged director.

With Raj Khosla and his point of view about dialogues out of the way, Abrar had the field to himself. He set about his job with new gusto, like a man inspired. No more arguing at every point, over every line. His views on the subject amount to an impromptu lesson in effective dialogue writing.

∽

I stuck to my view that dialogue reflects the personality of a character. And personality is the sum total of a person's or character's environment, upbringing, education and background. Companions, mental abilities and his own turn of phrase also add colour to how a person speaks.

A writer has to know a character as well as a mother knows her children. Just as a mother knows, when she turns around and glares with angry eyes at two of her children who are making mischief in some corner of the room, that one of them will cower in fear and the other will stick his tongue out at her, so also the writer must know how each of his characters will react to any situation. From that knowledge good dialogues emerge.

Putting this premise to practice, I created five different languages or rather versions of Hindi for the five key characters in *Aar Paar*.

The film had been floated with Geeta Bali and Guru Dutt even before I came into the scene. When Geeta Bali bowed out, before the shooting began, Shyama was signed on. The script included a strong Punjabi character in the heroine's father; a Parsi comedian; the hero—a taxi driver, living in Bombay but hailing from Madhya Pradesh (MP) or the then Central Provinces; and a Qazi friend of the heroine's father, who originally hailed from Lucknow.

I knew they were all placed in Bombay where the film was located, but I also knew from real life that living in a cosmopolitan city does not always remove from one's speech all traces of the language one has grown up with. Inflections, accents and turn of phrase can more often than not indicate a person's origin or roots.

I gave each character idioms particular to his or her background. Thus when the heroine's father scolds Guru Dutt, the illiterate taxi driver who has grown up in a village in MP responds, '*Bakat bakat ki baat hai lalaji, aaj yaaron ka bakat dheela hai is liye garaj ke bolte hai* . . .' I made him say 'bakat' rather than 'waqt', and 'yaaron' instead of 'mera' . . . I think it added a large dose of authenticity to his character.

Again, Johnny Walker who plays the Parsi comedian says in typical Parsi-speak, '*Main tumko pehleich bola tum udhar se chaloni karke* . . .' 'Karke' is such a typical Bombay Hindi phrase.

Thus *Aar Paar* became, for the first time in Hindi films, a mirror of the melting pot of tongues that a city could be.

In a scene where the heroine's father, played by Jagdish Sethi, and his friend, the Qazi from Lucknow, played by character actor Rajinder, are playing chess, a game Abrar himself enjoyed, the lights suddenly go out.

The host goes to get candles, at which point the Qazi quickly moves a horse on the board. Peering at the board by candlelight, Sethi exclaims that his horse has been moved. His friend insists that the horse was exactly there; it had been there right through.

The Lalaji gets angry. '*Shatranjwich beimani karta hai, doon kya ek laafa . . .?*' he asks in typical Punjabi wrath.

The Qazi backs down to his Lucknavi roots. '*Shatranj dimagi khel hai janaab,*' he drawls. After a string of exclamations in chaste Urdu, he ends, '*Dimagi khel mein haata pai ki kya zaroorat hai?*'

And in the same vein, Uma Devi, who portrays a typical Bombay Christian in Guru Dutt's *Mr and Mrs '55*, also written by Abrar Alvi, says, '*Khali pili kyon bom marta hai?*' Probably the precursor of all such dialogues that typecast the Goan Christian in Hindi films for evermore.

But Abrar's association with *Aar Paar* was not limited to writing dialogues. There was another important aspect of the film Abrar was involved with, a responsibility he would be entrusted with in every subsequent Guru Dutt film.

❦

My interaction with Guru Dutt in *Aar Paar* went beyond just writing dialogues. As he had laid down right at the beginning, when he first decided to hire me, I was to be present on the sets every day, and was to give the artists their lines. Guru Dutt was yet to develop his acting skills, he was very limited in histrionic ability at the time. Knowing that I had been a radio artist as a voice for radio plays and could not only write and act on radio but could also direct both on radio and stage, Guru Dutt often took his cues from me.

He would stand facing a corner, his arm at right angles in a way that his elbow stuck out, his forearm across his eyes as he rested it against the wall, and call out, 'Abrar, how do I say the dialogue?' I would give him his lines, complete with inflections, and he would listen intently, eyes closed, still facing the wall, and when we were done, would take on the scene.

❦

It was during *Aar Paar* that both Abrar Alvi and Guru Dutt realized that fate had probably played a hand in bringing them together. It was quite a casual thing. They were at Shyama's house and Guru

Dutt, who had a whimsical interest in astrology, asked an astrologer who happened to be present to check out his future. He wanted to know if the film he was working on would succeed. *Baaz* had not fared too well, would *Aar Paar* change his luck?

∾

It was strange. Here he was asking these questions. I was agnostic by nature and did not believe in astrology and things like that. But I listened out of sheer curiosity. The pundit cast Guru Dutt's horoscope and looked at it intently.

I knew Guru Dutt had had his horoscope already cast. In fact, he had mine made too, when he discovered we were both Cancerians. He was born on the ninth of July; I was born on the first. He had seemed pleased when he discovered the fact. 'Nine plus one makes ten,' he had said, 'and ten is a powerful number.'

That day, Guru Dutt asked me to go and wait in his car as he wanted to talk to the pundit privately. I learnt of his conversation with the astrologer only when he came down to join me in the car. As we drove off, he told me the pundit had looked at his horoscope and said, 'This is a good horoscope, and at least for ten years you don't have to worry, you will have a good life.'

'What happens after ten years?' Guru Dutt had asked with the curiosity that was such an intrinsic part of his nature. The same curiosity that made him watch chickens hatching in an incubator, or propelled him to try ploughing a field so he could know what it felt like to drive a plough through the earth.

The pundit had looked him squarely in the eyes and said, 'After ten years, I can see a great turmoil. I can see upheaval. And I see a break in this partnership.'

By all accounts, this was a professional reading. It was pertinent to his career, and the ups and downs of life in a typically unstable environment like films. I did not give his words any credence, but events were to make me believe in the power of astrology.

❧

The year was 1954, and Guru Dutt, at the start of his career, had much to look forward to. In fact, as prophesied, he moved from strength to strength. *Aar Paar* did quite well, and his next film, *Mr and Mrs '55*, established him as a maker of fine comedy films. *Pyaasa* placed him firmly in the league of all-time greats. There was no reason to believe that, despite the dismal performance of *Kaagaz Ke Phool* at the box office, he was not one of cinema's most creative forces.

But exactly ten years after the pundit had made his prediction, Guru Dutt's life took a sudden turn. The year was 1964. In October, Guru Dutt died. Abrar's ten-year partnership with him was over.

7

Kaheka Jhagda Baalam
Nayi Nayi Preet Re

With *Aar Paar* the battle of wits between two intellects had begun. When the film, with its action-packed climax, was released, it ran triumphantly for twenty-two weeks. Unwilling to let go of the opportunity, Guru Dutt taunted Abrar that the film had done so well only because he had put in the action scenes at the climax. Not one to be cowed down, Abrar retorted that if he had maintained the emotional climax, the film would probably have clocked thirty-two weeks!

But even as the two bantered among themselves and revelled in the success of the film, unknown to Abrar, his fate was being decided by someone who felt that Abrar could threaten the very success of Guru Dutt Films—K.K. Kapoor, the film's producer. After the success of *Aar Paar*, Kapoor took his director on a tour of Europe. They were away for about ten days.

৽

I fancy Guru Dutt took Kapoor's lifestyle in his stride and, like a typical tourist, enjoyed the pleasures the tour offered. But all the time, even as he travelled, his mind was constantly on the alert for a new subject, filing away ideas, sights, impressions . . . his thirst for cinema was constant.

When he returned, Guru Dutt was all set, eager to start his next film. I was called for the sittings and told to take forward the work he had done in Europe. The sittings were in Kapoor's air-conditioned bungalow in Juhu.

Guru Dutt etched out his story idea to me. It was set in Goa. The hero was a smuggler of liquor, who of course had his own den. Two young men—freedom fighters for Goa's liberation from the Portuguese—hide in the den, and somewhere along the way, thanks to the heroine, who also is sympathetic towards the liberation movement, the hero gets reformed.

I was aghast. This would only be a continuation of Guru Dutt's swashbuckling, meaningless films reflecting his fascination for Goa. I knew why he was fond of the genre. Gyan Mukherjee, his guru, had made such films. *Kismet*, directed by Mukherjee, had been a super hit and had run for 108 weeks at Roxy, creating a world record. Guru Dutt was hoping to follow in his master's footsteps. But I had little patience with his fascination for the cloak-and-dagger stuff.

I turned to him after he had finished narrating his idea and asked him, 'Will you never be anything but a smuggler?'

K.K. Kapoor told me to shut up. 'This is what the public expects from Guru Dutt,' he said. Kapoor went on to hold up Hitchcock as an example of a director who had made only one kind of film throughout his career, and had attained a great measure of greatness, thanks to it.

I remember my repartee. I said, 'Mr Kapoor, there is a saying in English: exceptions prove the rule. Hitchcock is the exception. Against that I can cite so many examples of directors who are in the same league, like Cecil de Mille, John Huston, Billy Wilder, who have tremendous range, and tackle everything from the wild west to history to drama.'

All through my speech Guru Dutt was listening quietly. Now he said softly, '*Abrar theek toh kehta hai* . . . (Abrar is correct . . .)'

❧

And the die was cast.

K.K. Kapoor had always viewed with deep suspicion the influence the new writer seemed to wield on his director. Seeing how close Guru Dutt had come to changing the action climax of *Aar Paar* to an emotional one, he had decided that if he wanted to retain control over his productions and keep them tailored to the needs of the box office, Guru Dutt had to be weaned away from his writer's influence.

Kapoor told Guru Dutt he was certain that Abrar Alvi was 'a very dangerous and corrupting influence' and should not be entertained for future projects. Guru Dutt did not have much of a choice but to concur with his producer's diktat. So, when he went across for discussions on future enterprises, Abrar sat around in his office doing little. 'Luckily for me, Guru Dutt did not ask me to stop attending office, so I was not really out of a job, only out of work,' he says.

The exile was, however, as short-lived as it was bitter. Abrar tells it with a sense of drama.

❧

For all practical purposes, to K.K. Kapoor I was insignificant and as such should have no opinion. I was of no importance at all, and it was no problem for him to brush off a nonentity like me. I don't think he gave it any great consideration, he wanted me out of the way, and that was that. Now, given my confrontational views on the next film he was planning with Guru Dutt, he decided to give his diktat: I was not welcome at his bungalow and was not to attend the sittings.

But, one evening, a few days later, Guru Dutt came in his car and picked me up. We drove on to Marine Drive to meet Shakila.

I had not seen him in such a mood before. He raved and ranted, and kept talking about KK. As I listened patiently, trying to fathom what had caused his ire, I realized that he had had a falling out with Kapoor.

The crux of the matter was that Guru Dutt had told KK that he might be the producer, but that did not give him the right to interfere with the subject. Even the fact that he was to make two more films for KK did not give him that right.

Suddenly he turned to me. 'You say you are a writer . . . tell me, do you have a subject you can develop into a screenplay for me?'

The challenge was one I could not ignore. I thrashed about in my mind for a brief while and then pulled out from my memory a play I had written and directed to great effect in college. The play was titled *A Modern Marriage*. I narrated a scene to him briefly. He seemed to like what he heard.

Guru Dutt was actually quite fascinated by the character of the lovable idiot who was the heroine of my play. Perhaps the challenge of breaking the norm and having a less than perfect heroine appealed to him. He asked me if I could develop the character and do a story around her. I said I could.

He told me to go right ahead and develop the screenplay. However, he had a contribution to make. Guru Dutt had seen the James Stewart–Hedy Lamarr film *Come Live with Me*. He was quite keen on blending some aspects of that film into the script, which I did.

It is true that I was a fledgling writer, and he was a director who was well into finding his directorial voice. But the fact remains that Guru Dutt never really acknowledged publicly or in the film credits the extent of my contribution to this film.

A *Modern Marriage* was the story of an impetuous, lovable but slightly foolish young woman who marries so as to inherit a fortune that could be hers only on her marriage. It was Guru Dutt's first brush with comedy, and helped him in his search for his métier as a director. *Mr and Mrs '55* also introduced Madhubala as an actress capable of handling comedy. Luckily for both writer and director, the star was suitably impressed with Abrar's rendition of her role, and thoroughly enjoyed playing the part of Mrs '55. And the Madhubala–Abrar mutual fan club continued beyond the film. Abrar smiles at some half-forgotten memories as he goes down the road to *Mr and Mrs '55*.

When I approached Madhubala for the role, she was flabbergasted. She was already quite famous, her career had started when she was still a child, and she had grown from child artist to a regal, beautiful star. Her skin often broke out in acne, but the filters hid it well, but what they could not hide was her dazzling smile, which made her unique and set her apart.

Her repertoire, till *Mr and Mrs '55*, had been a host of serious films. The public considered her a 'serious' actress. I wanted to cast her as the 'lovable idiot' in *Mr and Mrs '55*. The role was completely foreign to her but Guru Dutt was keen on casting her and I too felt she could handle it well.

When we started shooting there were times when she would say, 'How can I do this? What is this?' But once she was walked through the scenes, which I did frequently with her, she got the nuances and enacted them with aplomb. Her timing was perfect. She knew exactly how to get a reaction from the audience and how long to hold that reaction.

❧

On the sets, Madhubala was a load of fun. She had an infectious laughter and a healthy sense of mischief. Abrar remembers Madhubala matching Guru Dutt in mischief, trick for trick, but while Guru Dutt was engrossed in the making of the film, his heroine had plenty of time to amuse herself. Though she was a thorough professional, she was also very conscious of her need to be the only star in the film, and was always wary of someone stealing a scene or the limelight away from her.

Thus it was that whenever Kumkum's sister, who played the role of a secretary, had to cry for a very important scene, Madhubala would start laughing loudly. Peal after peal of loud, full-throated laughter that would not only distract everybody on the sets, but also ruin the mood for the actress emoting the scene. At every retake she would start laughing, ensuring that it would lead to another take.

❧

I was only one film old, and had little stature, but as the film progressed, Madhubala grew to respect me as someone qualified enough to bring out hidden depths in any artist. By the time we finished the film, she had come to realize that she could be a great comic artist too.

Later, when I was shooting for *Pyaasa*, Madhubala sent for me one day. I went across to her house and she gave me some money and said, 'This is for you to write a film for me. I have a liking for comedy now and I will direct it, if you write it and are present on the sets while it is being made.'

What surprised me even more was that she already had a central idea for the film's story. 'I want you to reverse the boy-loves-girl-and-parents-oppose-it theme,' she said. 'I want the parents of the hero and the heroine planning to get them married to each other, and the two trying their best to get out of the situation by making their parents become enemies. But in the process of planning this, they fall in love. Of course by the time they realize their feelings for each other, their ruse has succeeded and their parents have fallen out, and are hell-bent on opposing their marriage.'

It was a fun theme, and would have made a great film, but it was not to be. Madhubala agreed to wait till *Pyaasa* was completed as I was fully committed to Guru Dutt Films and the movie. By the time *Pyaasa* was finished, Madhubala was a very sick woman, though she did not know it herself.

While on a shoot in Madras, she suddenly vomited blood, and that was when her severe heart condition became public. She was advised medically against directing a film, it would be much too strenuous and thus a life-threatening activity for her, so the film was never made.

∽

Curiously enough, a film with a similar theme was made in 1959. The film, *Chacha Zindabad*, a hilarious comedy, was directed by J. Om Prakash. It is interesting to ponder where the idea for the film originated, considering that it starred Kishore Kumar, Madhubala's husband in her last years and her co-star in a number of hit films of the period.

8

Janam Safal Ho Jaaye

Two women totally unconnected and unknown to each other contributed to making *Pyaasa* the classic it is: Gulabo and Waheeda Rehman. Abrar Alvi met Gulabo quite by accident. And Waheeda came to Guru Dutt Films as a vamp, thanks to a buffalo. Two stories that Abrar recounts in great detail and with emotion.

I was writing *Aar Paar*. I was still staying as a guest with cousin Yashwant, who was by then seriously considering marrying his paramour, the vivacious ex-partner of Haridarshan Films. (He did marry Haridarshan Kaur, and their daughter, Yogeeta Bali, became an actress in the 1970s.)

I had some rich friends from Hyderabad. They had studied with me in Nagpur and some of them had stayed at the YMCA as I did. We had kept in touch. They had driven down from Hyderabad to Bombay for a bit of fun, and when they found out where I was, and that I was 'in the film line', it excited their curiosity. They drove across town to meet me.

I had no place even to seat them, let alone entertain them in the way they were used to being entertained. I tried to take them across the road to the Irani hotel, but they insisted I get into their car and drove away with me saying, 'Have dinner with us, we will drop you back at night.'

We drove to the seashore. There were many shacks there, built for couples who needed to meet clandestinely. My friends had rented one of those. The place has developed now and the well-known Janki Kutir residential complex stands in place of the shacks, but those days it was lonely and quiet and the air was sonorous with the swishing of palm leaves.

They had prepared well for the evening. There were bottles of rum, and glasses, food and clean plates. I was a little ill at ease, having never had alcohol till then. But I was happy to be with old friends again, and they were a hospitable lot, so I was soon engrossed in their conversation.

Then, as the evening wore on, suddenly I could hear some giggling behind the cloth curtain, and before I could ask what the matter was, the curtain moved aside and three or four girls entered the room where we were sitting. They came and sat amongst us. They must have been about fifteen or sixteen and there was an older woman in charge of them, twenty-eight or twenty-nine perhaps. Or maybe she was younger . . .

I was at sea. I was, as they say, an *anari*. My friends, being sons of zamindars, were veterans in the habit of visiting kothas, interacting with women. I was shocked when they asked me to take my pick of the girls. I was still celibate, I had never known a woman before. Even though I had finally been tempted into taking a few sips of liquor, I was still in my senses to be able to refuse this offer. But they would not let up. I was their guest, they said, and I had to pick my woman first; only after I had made my choice could they pair up with the rest.

I continued to demur, then finally driven to pique by their insistence, I pointed to the oldest one. She was aghast at my choice.

'Why pick me when there are all these young, nubile women here?' she exclaimed.

I stuck to my choice, and the others paired up and went off to the beach, 'to have some fun'. The evening turned into night, and as the night rolled on, my friends floated in and out of the shack. The woman I had picked stayed in the shack with me. We talked. Her name, I discovered, was Gulabo. And I found her interesting.

∾

Abrar was to keep in touch with Gulabo for more than three years. She left a deep enough impression on him to inspire him to create one of Hindi cinema's most unforgettable characters.

The first glimpse of Gulabo in *Pyaasa* is deceptive. She stands with her back to the camera, wrapped in a diaphanous sari. Her head is demurely covered. And it is only when she breaks into a song, and turns to look coyly back at Guru Dutt and lead him on, that you realize there is coquetry under the apparent demureness.

As the movie unravels, Gulabo proves to be a woman very different from the preconceived image of a streetwalker. A certain dignity combined with her adoration of the poet whose songs she has taken into her heart give her the grit and determination to fight for his cause and decide to be by his side, for better or worse.

Though *Pyaasa* has sterling performances by each of its artists, it is the character of Gulabo that stands out and reaches close to the stature of the hero. And yet, Gulabo was nowhere in the scheme of things when Guru Dutt first thought of his next film, says Abrar, talking of the time before *Pyaasa* was conceived.

∾

He did have a theme he wanted to explore. Guru Dutt had in mind the character of a rich, powerful socialite, a woman who was a patron of the arts and young artists. She would pick up the most promising one, and build him up, then dump him for a new interest. Through this process she would promote herself. The hero of the film would be one such artist, who would get involved with her, but would walk out of the tangle before she could dump him.

The idea had been triggered by the Chetana Art Gallery in Kala Ghoda, Bombay. Guru Dutt had probably modelled the socialite on Chhaya Arya (who incidentally runs the gallery now; it sells clothes by artisans, rather than fine art these days), whose father owned the gallery, and built a story around her, creating out of a person and a situation an imagined persona.

∞

At the time that Guru Dutt was toying with this theme of the rich socialite gallery owner, Abrar had known Gulabo for all of three years. She was, by then, weighing heavy on his conscience. And he felt he had let her down as only a man could let a woman down, a woman who was dependent on him.

Abrar's interest in Gulabo had begun as curiosity. He was a writer after all, and here was his chance of understanding the psyche of a woman of uncertain character from close quarters. That evening when his friends had left the two of them together in the shack, Abrar started a conversation with his companion— as much to hold her attentions at bay as to satiate his curiosity about her kind.

By the time the revelries ended, Abrar had spent the better part of the night talking to Gulabo. It was almost six in the morning when the party broke up, and all of them piled into the car, the men as well as the girls, who would be dropped off on the way.

'Gulabo insisted I walk her to the car,' Abrar remembers. 'Then as I stepped back to let her get into the car, she suddenly caught my wrist. "Come with me," she said, "we can talk some more on the way." I pointed out to her that there was little room in the car. "Sit on my lap," she offered.'

Abrar laughs reliving the moment of utter shock. 'She laughed at my discomfiture,' he says, 'but I was persuaded to fit myself into the crush inside the car.'

He found the writer in him drawn to Gulabo. They worked out a novel method of meeting. Gulabo lived at Teli Gali, Lalbaug, in Parel. Abrar's memory is crystal clear on the details: 'It is the first gali right of the bus station.' Her place of work, however, was in a brothel in Murgi Gali, which is parallel to the Grant Road Bridge.

She had a sharp tongue and a sharper sense of humour. She had the capacity to take me by surprise. There was so much depth in her. I was drawn to meeting her repeatedly, over a period of time. I used to enjoy her company. We would spend the time talking of this and that. I learnt the story of her life in those meetings.

Once, when I had dropped in to see her, one of the other girls, who was actually her rival in the business, told me she was out. I turned to leave, but she beckoned me to stay, and started to lead me into an inner room. I demurred, saying I would come back for Gulabo later, another time, another day.

Gulabo must have been in the room next to the one I was standing in. She heard my voice, and in minutes, she stood there like a wild tigress. She pounced on her rival, telling her to keep off her customer, meaning me, and before I knew it the two women were at each other's throats, tearing and scratching like two cats.

I fled the scene, hurrying away as fast as I could. But Gulabo came running after me and caught up with me. Stopping a taxi, she ushered me into it. I told her I could not afford a cab ride; she told me to be quiet, she did not expect me to pay. The taxi driver was instructed to drive us to some address she gave him in Elphinstone Road.

There, she made me sit in the taxi, while she entered a building. She must have arranged everything to her satisfaction, because she soon came back, and I still remember how miserable I felt as she paid the taxi driver and led me into the building, guiding me up a flight of stairs into a dimly lit room, with only a bed in it.

We sat there, talking, as if it was the most natural thing to do. Suddenly there was a knock on the door. I started, afraid of what would follow. But she opened the door a crack, and someone thrust a packet into her hand. She held it out to me, somewhat triumphantly, a quart bottle of Indian whisky wrapped in newspaper.

It was the same night that, as we talked and drank, I think I saw a Gulabo I had not seen before. She sat against the wall, her hair loose, legs drawn up on the bed, while I sat a little distance away, taking sips from my glass.

At some point, I remember letting loose a string of invectives, at which she leaned forward and shut my mouth with her hand. I was surprised. 'Why did you stop me?' I asked. 'You use these words yourself . . .'

She looked at me for a moment, then rolled her head against the wall, closing her eyes with her arm. 'I am a loose woman, a prostitute,' she said, 'but you are not like me. Such words do not sound good from your mouth . . .' And the look she gave me beseeched me not to fall from her esteem, not to topple from the pedestal she had placed me on.

The room on Elphinstone Road soon became our meeting place. Each time I visited her at the brothel, I would have to pay thirty rupees to be able to see her. She worked out a way to save me from spending that money. 'Show me your face and then go and stand at the nearby shop and enjoy a smoke,' she said, 'I will come there in ten minutes.'

She would hurry to join me, looking quickly over her shoulder to see whether she was being followed, and then she would take me to Elphinstone Road. The first time we went there after that strange night, I confessed that I had a little money on me, but she shut me up. We would sit there and she would order food, and we would eat. She would serve me, insisting that I try this dish and that. And all the time we would talk. She would pay for the meal, and we would end up talking through the night.

It was something I can never forget, the way she fed me. And I translated it directly from my life into *Pyaasa*. I think she found me different because I was the first man to treat her like a human being, to talk to her, to even try and hold a proper conversation with her. She had a deep thirst for knowledge, and would ply me with questions. Of course she had imbibed some of her trade's habits. She could be loud and foul-mouthed; her gaalis might have even made a sailor blush.

Gulabo, Abrar discovered, was not born into the profession she now practised. Over a span of meetings she revealed her story to him, a story as amazing as anything any scriptwriter ever wrote.

She was born into a Hindu family, the daughter of a Brahmin. She was still an adolescent when she encountered the strong, handsome policeman who rode through her village on his horse. The crush developed into an affair, and she eloped with him. By the time she found out that he was a married man, it was too late. When he finally ditched her, there was no way she could go back home to face her parents. As in most of these cases, her homelessness and good looks were noticed by a madam of a brothel, who gave her shelter and a livelihood. Her name, Devi, was changed to Gulabo, a screen behind which she could hide her origins and her identity.

As he got more deeply involved in the making of *Mr and Mrs '55*, Abrar's visits to Gulabo became irregular. In any case, Gulabo's need to see Abrar was stronger than his need to meet her. It was she who insisted on fixing a time and date for their next meeting, and Abrar would often miss the appointed time or day, busy as he was with his work at Guru Dutt Films. Work was a commitment with him and days would pass before he could find some spare time to take the bus to Murgi Gali. Thursdays were fixed for their meeting, but more often than not, weeks would come and go without the date being kept. 'There were times when I knew I was being hard on Gulabo, treating her with a cavalier attitude,' he says softly, 'but that was how it was, and now when I think of it I feel really guilty.' As he got more and more caught up in his work, his visits to Gulabo ceased altogether.

It must have been after almost an eight-month gap. A man came searching me out, saying he had come at her behest. She was sick, very sick, and she had sent him saying that he should bring me to see her. 'Tell him he must come,' she had said. So I went.

It was a complicated route to her house, but finally, after many twists and turns through narrow lanes, I found myself outside her house. The door was closed; there was a lock on it. I was about to turn away when a young girl came running up to me. She asked me if I was looking for Gulabo. I nodded, confused.

'My mother is very sick, my father has taken her to the doctor, she will be back soon,' she said, then added, 'she told me you might come today, and she wants you to wait for her return.'

The girl dusted a large stone lying nearby and made me sit on it.

I waited, and after a while I saw Gulabo walking up the lane. She ran towards me, stumbling when she saw me. I could see she was close to tears. I was aghast at her appearance. She had lost weight dramatically, her face was lined, and there was none of the sparkle that had set her apart.

I learned as she ushered me into her little house that she had been suffering from bouts of fever over the past few months and the doctor had diagnosed it as tuberculosis. But more than the illness, it was the fact that I had stopped coming to see her that hurt her, she said. Would I promise to come again, every Thursday, as I had done earlier?

I promised. I gave the money I had to her husband to ensure she would get her medicines regularly. I will come back with more money next Thursday, I promised.

She looked at me with large eyes, hollowed by fever and the wasting disease she was now in the grip of. 'You won't come,' she said, 'you are a busy man now, you will forget your Gulabo like you have done all these months, and when you do remember to come to see me, I will be dead.'

I took her hand in mine and promised her I would be there next week.

∾

It was a false promise. Involved deeply in his work, Abrar had little idea of how the months sped past. Abrar's eyes are moist as he narrates the story of Gulabo's prophesy coming true, and how his conscience will never let him forget the fact that he had neglected her at a time when she needed him the most.

∾

One evening Guru Dutt asked me to go and watch a film, and report to him on it the next day. I took a bus and went into town, to the cinema hall where the film was showing, and dutifully watched the film, making mental notes as I sat through the scenes. It was nine p.m. by the time the show ended. As it was a long ride back, I, as I was wont to do, went to the top of the double-decker and sat by the window.

The bus route went through Grant Road and it was when we turned into the road that I remembered Gulabo and realized with a start that it was Thursday. I thought for a moment about jumping off the bus and going across to see her. But it was late in the night, and there would be no more buses later. I hesitated, torn between the promise I had made and the practical considerations my mind put before me.

It was then that the bus halted. I looked out to see a funeral procession going past on that narrow road. I watched idly, and then, the unexpected hit. I saw, as the bier passed slowly by, that the face of the corpse it carried was uncovered. With a start, I realized that I was looking at Gulabo . . .

I narrated the story of Gulabo to Guru Dutt while we were still shooting for *Mr and Mrs '55*. We were spending an evening together after the shooting, drinking to ease the tiredness of the day's work, when suddenly I felt the need to talk. I narrated the entire story to him, in a rush.

Guru Dutt was quite captivated by her character, and asked me if I could make her the basis of a story. It was a challenge I felt I could take on. However, there were some things that needed to be sorted out. I told Guru Dutt that I would like to bring out the selflessness of the streetwalker by contrasting it with the selfish greed of the socialite character that he had thought of using in a film. It would go down well with the audience. But creating a script with the two disparate elements and making a screenplay of it would take a lot of time. Guru Dutt agreed to give me time. As the story evolved, other adjustments were made.

With a streetwalker as the heroine there was little chance of romance in the film. How would a film where the protagonists did not sing and dance together work? Guru Dutt decided to let passion take the place of romance, and to let the unsaid speak louder than words.

Because Gulabo's relationship with the film's protagonist was based on the real-life relationship Gulabo and I had shared, it was decided that the protagonist would not be a painter as originally planned but a writer. And to enable songs to be included in the movie, to let the director indulge his passion for picturizing song sequences, the writer would be a poet.

It was all settled. I transferred much of my relationship with Gulabo into the script, even taking some of her lines verbatim, and the rest was quite easy.

∽

But even as he worked on the script of the yet untitled film that would become a legend, Abrar got involved with *CID*.

9

Kahin Pe Nigahen,
Kahin Pe Nishana

If the character of Gulabo gave *Pyaasa* its cutting edge, the artist who played the role made her claim to being one of India's finest actors with her delineation of the streetwalker who stakes her all to fulfil a poet's dream of being published.

Even today, Waheeda Rehman admits that of all the roles she has essayed on screen, three count among her favourites. Two of these are in Guru Dutt's films, *Pyaasa* and *Kaagaz Ke Phool*, the third is the role of Rosie in Vijay Anand's *Guide*.

To Guru Dutt, however, goes the credit of discovering Waheeda Rehman. According to Abrar, it's a story worth telling. 'Waheeda has a buffalo to thank for the fact that we signed her on,' says Abrar Alvi, laughing at the memory, as his mind flips back to the time when Waheeda was still a starlet in the south, and Guru Dutt, idling between films, was impatiently looking for a new project.

∾

Mr and Mrs '55 was done, the screenplay of *Pyaasa* was being written, and Guru Dutt was impatient with the fact that he had no project to sink his teeth into. Besides, he was a bit unsure about the success of *Pyaasa*. The subject was serious and, after *Mr and Mrs '55*, a terrific departure from comedy. He wanted to keep in hand a lighter, frothier subject closer to the audiences' tastes, just to play safe.

It was at this time that a distributor from the south told us about a film, *Missiamma*, that was creating waves in Andhra Pradesh. It was a big hit, he averred, and remaking it in Hindi would give Guru Dutt a hat-trick of hits.

Guru Dutt was interested and demanded a print. But the distributor, Manu Bhai, suggested he go to Hyderabad, as the prints were all running in various theatres at that time. He also offered a translator's services in Hyderabad, which would be useful as the film was in Telugu.

Guru Dutt instructed me to take a flight to Hyderabad and watch the film. 'Report to me if there is a decent possibility of our remaking it,' he said.

But when our production controller, Guruswamy, tried to book me a ticket to Hyderabad, none was available. For some reason, the flights were completely booked for days on end. We tried for train tickets, but again none were available. I think it was the middle of the vacations.

Finally, it was decided that I would take Guru Dutt's Plymouth and drive down to Hyderabad. I told Guru Dutt, 'It's a big car, why don't you also come along?' and so he decided to drive with me, and we took Guruswamy along too. The plan was made at four in the afternoon, by nine-thirty we were off, driving via Sholapur to Hyderabad.

That was when fate stepped in, in the form of a buffalo.

The driver suffered from night blindness, but of course he had not told any of us about his ailment. He drove the car into a mound of rubbish. That was when we found out about his condition, and forced him to give the wheel to me. I drove right through the night, and we reached Hyderabad at about ten in the morning.

The driver then offered to take the wheel again, as it was day, but I continued to drive. Fatigue must have crept over me, which is why the accident happened. There was a cart with a buffalo tied to it, ahead of me. I tried to overtake the cart and, as I drew alongside, sounded my horn as a warning. Startled, the buffalo ran out, straight into the side of the car.

Luckily for all of us, and especially for the animal, the buffalo was not badly hurt. The car, however, was quite decidedly smashed. However, to prevent further trouble, we paid off the cart driver, and drove off as fast as the car could take us, crumpled side and all.

The garage we took it to assured us that the car was not beyond repair. The only issue was that the job would take between two to three days. Murdeshwar Rao, who had been assigned to escort us, was not dismayed. He saw this as a great opportunity to play host to Guru Dutt. He arranged a private screening of the film we had come to see. The film unfortunately did not impress Guru Dutt. Murdeshwar Rao now had to think up various ways of keeping us happy and entertained while the garage worked on making the car roadworthy again.

❧

As luck would have it, Guru Dutt, Abrar and Guruswamy landed up at the offices of a distributor at Secunderabad. He was a friend of Murdeshwar Rao, and Guru Dutt decided to pay him a courtesy call. As they chatted, fate played its hand again.

❧

We were idly looking out of the door and talking among ourselves, when a car drew up with a group of urchins trailing behind it. A woman got out and, avoiding the young boys crowding around her, entered the building opposite ours. I asked the distributor, 'Is there an office there, who is that woman?' He replied, 'She is a dancer in a Telugu film *Rojulu Marayi*, which is a super hit thanks to her dance number.' The film was celebrating its hundredth day and the starlet had become so popular that film goers had started recognizing her, which was also the reason the urchins were running after her car, he explained.

The distributor of *Rojulu Marayi* had his office opposite where we were sitting and that is where the starlet had gone. I asked what her name was, and our host answered, 'Waheeda Rehman.' I was intrigued by the Muslim name, and he told me she was a Telugu Muslim girl from Bezwada (present-day Vijayawada).

I asked if she could speak Hindi. She could, he said. 'Would Guru Dutt like to meet her?' he suggested. Guru Dutt said why not, anyway we had time to kill. The distributor sent word across the road, and in a little while, she came over to meet us.

It was an anticlimax. She was very plainly dressed, without even lipstick to relieve the monotony of her face, strangely reserved, and spoke softly in near monosyllables in response to our small talk and queries. Then, getting up abruptly, she folded her hands into a namaste, and said, '*Ab main chaloongi*,' in a markedly south Indian accent, and turned and left.

∼

In short, there was little in that meeting to suggest that Guru Dutt Films had just encountered its biggest star.

The distributor, however, pushed her case. He persuaded Guru Dutt and his companions to watch the starlet's dance number. Again, more to kill time than out of any real desire to watch the starlet they had just met, the trio agreed. Needless to say, the reel was not available right away. It had to be arranged, a hall had to be fixed for the viewing, and while all that was being done post-haste, the friends spent the afternoon quaffing beer and having lunch.

～

By the time we got to the projection room we had downed six bottles, and, more likely than not, were in a happy haze.

The reel was shown, the dance number was fast paced and well executed, but there was not a single shot of the dancer in close-up. 'How is she?' Guru Dutt asked at the end of it. 'Very photogenic,' I replied. 'I also think so,' Guru Dutt opined. And we asked the distributor to arrange a meeting.

Once the car was repaired and we went back, we forgot all about Waheeda for the time being. All that remained in memory was that we had made a fruitless trip to see a film called *Missiamma* which we had not liked. And Guru Dutt was exactly in the same position he had been before the trip. Restless and wondering what to take up next as a foil to *Pyaasa*.

～

Missiamma was made into a Hindi film but not by Guru Dutt. The Hindi version, *Miss Mary*, starred Meena Kumari and went on to become a hit. Guru Dutt, meanwhile, focussed on a new theme that seemed to catch his fancy. It was called *The Man with My Face*.

10

Kaahe Ghabraye?

Time was running out, so was money. The unit members of Guru Dutt Films had to be paid their salaries regardless of whether there was work or not; they were on the rolls of the company after all. The need of the moment was to get a film on the floors.

Guru Dutt decided to do a double bill. On the one hand he let the story of the streetwalker spin itself out, and on the other, because he worried that the theme was too offbeat and thus could fail to win the audience, he toyed with the idea of launching another project which would be a definite box-office draw.

The venture: a thriller based on the English film *The Man with My Face*.

Guru Dutt's erstwhile assistant, Raj Khosla, was asked to direct the new movie. One offshoot of this was that Atma Ram, Guru Dutt's brother and chief assistant in *Mr and Mrs '55*, got seriously piqued at being bypassed and the director's cap being given to Khosla. In a huff, he took up a job in the Burmah Shell Film Unit which handled the documentaries and publicity for Burmah Shell. He would work with Guru Dutt Films only years later.

The new film was titled *CID*. It had everything people expected of a typical Guru Dutt film: the mandatory smuggler's den, an innocent, wide-eyed heroine and a gangster's moll. Shakila had been signed on to play the heroine. It was while casting for the vamp, who would have to sing and seduce the hero, that Guru Dutt remembered the Telugu film starlet he had met briefly in Hyderabad. He remembered too that Abrar Alvi had also liked her and had commented that she would be quite good if they could clean up her diction.

Manu Bhai, Guru Dutt's distributor for the Mysore and Hyderabad territories, was asked to draw up a contract with Waheeda Rehman. He was quite close to Guru Dutt, who regarded him as a friend and decided he was the right man for the job. Abrar remembers Guru Dutt saying that the wise thing to do would be to put the actress on a three-year contract (it was finally drawn up for five years). She could then be cast in both films on hand, and would be a comparatively low-cost proposition, being a newcomer. Knowing Guru Dutt's penchant for cabarets and song-and-dance numbers, there would be enough work for her in both films.

Waheeda shifted to Bombay and was given a flat near Guru Dutt's house, where she lived with her mother, her sister Sayeeda and her brother-in-law, Rauf. She was told that she would play the role of the vamp in *CID*.

Though he was not directly involved in either the writing or the direction of *CID*, and continued to work on the story of the streetwalker, Abrar functioned as an informal consultant on the script and was also given the task of breaking in Waheeda.

❧

I remember going to Waheeda with a list of screen names that I wanted her to choose from and adopt. Waheeda, we felt, was not a very filmi name; a film magazine had already got the name wrong and called her Wadia Rehman. But Waheeda was a girl with a mind of her own. She refused to look at the list and was adamant about not changing her name! So, Waheeda it was that went on the titles of *CID*.

Waheeda's face was photogenic, but it was a calm and homely face, not the face of a temptress, as the script demanded. Thus, as it went along, we had to change the script to accommodate Waheeda's looks.

Abrar took upon himself the task of rewriting the scenes where Waheeda featured, to add credibility to her character. As the film progressed, she was no longer the vamp. Instead, at risk to her own life, she warns the hero of the trap laid for him, and endears herself to the audience so that they accept the fact that the hero could have a place in his heart for her.

As it happened, I ended up writing the climax of *CID* which was a court scene. I played a role in the scene too. Inder Raj Anand was given the task of writing the film. I was asked to sit in, and give my ideas and opinions. When the climax was being worked out, Inder Raj Anand turned to me and said, 'I do not know what Guru Dutt wants. You understand him better, sit with him and try to understand what he wants before he gets irritated . . .' A group of people worked out possible alternatives, and before long I had taken over the climax of the film, dialogues and all.

The ending of *CID* was unusual. I took a gamble and suggested an end that was inspired by the many Hollywood films I had seen. I wasn't sure whether it would be accepted by the public. Guru Dutt liked it, so we went ahead and shot the ending. Luckily, the public also took kindly to it.

～

The ending of *CID*, for those who have not seen the film, has the hero, Dev Anand, standing confused between the two women in his life. On the one side is his sweetheart, Shakila, and on the other, Waheeda, the moll with a heart of gold who had saved his life. The film ended without letting the audience know the hero's choice. To the credit of all concerned with the making of the film, *CID* has enchanted three generations of viewers and continues to run to packed matinee shows in small towns even today. Waheeda's role in *CID* was brief, but she got noticed as an actress of promise—a promise she more than fulfilled with her next film, which was being written at the time.

In keeping with Guru Dutt's preference to go from one project to the next with the minimum amount of delay, within three weeks of the storyline being finalized, Gulabo's story went on the sets. Abrar's memories of his first days of working with an actress who would win laurels for her talent and maturity are worth recounting. He speaks about the entire exercise, tongue firmly in cheek.

～

I had suggested the name *Pyas*. The title would signify the thirst the protagonist has for fame and success. Guru Dutt suggested we change it to *Pyaasa*, which would indicate the character of the hero, rather than an abstract situation. So *Pyaasa* it was.

I was asked to rehearse Waheeda for her very first shot, and Guru Dutt, in all his wisdom, had chosen a dramatic scene to break in his new find. The first scene with which he started a new girl off was this: a customer after having a good time with a streetwalker throws her out of his horse carriage . . .

I told Guru Dutt, 'Why are you beginning with such a scene, she has never worked in Hindi before.' He had other views though. 'This will do away with her *hichak*,' he said. So I had no option.

She was sitting on a sofa. Guru Dutt was behind a table, on his chair. I was asked to sit next to her. The dialogue was, *Meri jaan* etc . . . in that vein, and I started speaking the dialogues for her to get the gist of the scene. Guru Dutt said, 'What is this straight delivery? Pull her by the shoulder as you speak.' I looked at him, he remained impassive. Flummoxed, I did as told. Waheeda was not amused.

Since *Aar Paar* I had been on a monthly salary with Guru Dutt Films, and part of my job was to be present on the sets at all times, look at the shots, tell the actors the mood, and give them their dialogues. Till I okayed the shot, it was not finalized. I also had the right to cut a shot. Sometimes, because of the way I intervened, visitors used to think I was the director.

When shooting actually started, Guru Dutt said, 'Prepare Waheeda for the role, get the dialogues done, get her on the floor ready to shoot.' She was in the make-up room. The make-up man said she was ready, only retouching was needed before the shot. I told him, 'You can do that even on the sets, now I need to give her the dialogues.' Then I turned to her and said, 'Waheeda-ji (later I would start calling her Waheeda, because I became sort of an elder brother), your first scene is a romantic one . . .'

I was sitting on a sofa near the make-up table; there was a stool next to it. She said, '*Ji, soonti hoon*,' and, picking up the stool, went to the farthest corner of the room from the sofa, set it down, then sat on it. Maybe the memory of our rehearsal a few weeks ago inspired her to act this way . . .

I said, 'Waheeda-ji, *romantic scene hai*.' She said, '*Bataiye . . .*' I said, 'A romantic scene needs soft tones . . . you are at such a great distance, do you want me to shout?'

When she refused to budge I went off in a huff. I went to Guru Dutt and said, 'I cannot do this, I cannot explain the scene to her . . . she goes a mile away to rehearse a romantic scene; am I to shout the lines?'

Guru Dutt remained calm and urged me to try once more. Somehow we managed to get her to rehearse the dialogue before getting on to the set.

11

Jinhe Naaz Hai Hind Par
Woh Kahan Hain

The stories that surround the making of what is today considered one of Hindi cinema's finest and most poetic compositions, *Pyaasa*, are legion. Eventually, the film's commercial success went beyond even the director's own expectations, but while it was under production, there was much anxiety and soul searching that went into it.

It is apparent that Guru Dutt, once he had the story of the film clear in front of him, knew the tone and shape he wanted the film to take. The market diktat of having songs and dances in films suited Guru Dutt, who enjoyed nothing as much as picturizing songs. As Abrar Alvi mentioned earlier, to accommodate the songs, the protagonist, though based on Abrar himself, would not be a writer, but a poet—the metre of poetry lends itself more easily to the rhythms of music.

As the director and Abrar Alvi got more deeply involved with the creation of *Pyaasa*, sitting through evenings and brainstorming became a habit, one that the director–writer duo would follow for many years to come.

Guru Dutt's mind was like a magpie's, going by Abrar's view

of the director. He would pick up bits and pieces—a scene here, a song idea there—and store them for the future. For example, he was enamoured of a 'chakla' of Sahir Ludhianvi's, and kept saying that some day he would like to use it in one of his films. Of course, he needed to find the right situation for it.

It was a visit to a kotha that gave Guru Dutt the right setting for Sahir's poem. This was during the trip to Hyderabad, at a time when the streetwalker project was yet to be finalized and Guru Dutt was still toying with the idea. It was Guru Dutt's first-ever visit to a kotha and, as Abrar mentions, it proved instrumental in Guru Dutt making up his mind on pursuing the project.

❧

Early in the discussions on *Pyaasa*, it was decided that the film would have a kotha as a background. There was only one problem: Guru Dutt had never been to a kotha . . . he was not the type at all. I had been to a kotha once, as a lark, with Raj Khosla, while we were both assistants to Guru Dutt. Raj had taken me one evening saying, '*Chalo gaana sunte hain.*'

Then in Hyderabad, we had nothing to do after we had seen *Missiamma* and watched Waheeda in the dance sequence in *Rojulu Marayi*, and while we waited for the car to be repaired. Murdeshwar Rao, a colourful personality, with his many ruby and diamond rings and his love of life, decided he would entertain Guru Dutt in the way the aristocrats of the city were used to by taking him to a kotha.

Guru Dutt was very hesitant. He was after all a known face, the hero of three or four films by then, some of which had been hits. But Rao swung him around by saying it would be a first-hand experience of a kotha, and thus offer a valuable insight. He bundled us into his car and took us to watch the dancing girls in action.

We reached the kotha; Rao had obviously been there before. He walked up the stairs and we followed. When the *baiji* appeared, Rao whispered something to her in Telugu. He must have told her he had important guests with him, for once we were in, the door was closed behind us.

Guru Dutt did not utter a word. He sat down to listen and notice. The responsibility of conversation was given to me. I listened as Murdeshwar Rao took upon himself the bargaining—he was half a Nizam in demeanour and style—and after a while I interrupted, saying, 'Let us listen to something.'

There were two girls in the room, the madam sat behind them, and once they saw we were at ease, one of the two girls started singing. To my surprise the song she selected was '*Kabhi aar, kabhi paar . . .*', and we knew then that Guru Dutt had been recognized. Guru Dutt looked at me, I looked at him, then I told the girl to stop singing after she had finished the mukhda. We had hoped to hide our identity, but had been caught out. We had to make the best we could of the evening, though. Whatever else, we did not want film songs coming out of our ears when we left.

The madam was quick to note our reactions. She asked us what we wanted to hear. I replied that we would like to hear something classical, a dadra, or thumri, or kajri. 'What the *theth* UP-walas listen to,' I said. The madam made a movement with her head and the girl started singing a thumri. She must have sung for twenty minutes or so, when there was a loud hammering on the door.

Someone rushed to open the door. Outside stood a very drunk man, looking like a filmi jagirdar, demanding to be let in. The singer said he was a regular patron, so he was allowed in. He entered with three other men and the door was quickly closed again.

He looked at the madam and asked, 'Who are these special people for whom you closed your door on me?' He was told that we were 'Bombay people'. I will never forget his looks. He was dressed in a shiny, yellow silk kurta with gota work on it, and the pyjama was of the same silk—it was as bright as the sun. He wore a maroon makhmal topi with gold work and silver edging, and his hands flashed with his battery of rings.

He studied us closely and soon realized that though I was doing most of the talking, I was always asking Guru Dutt first, and so he must be the most important man in the group. He turned to the singer and said, '*Ghazal sunao.*' She looked at us and started singing a ghazal. We knew then that that was the end of the thumri and kajri singing session for that evening.

As she sang, the man took out some money and placed it in front of him. The madam made a paan and sent it across with the second girl, who gave him the paan, picked up the money and returned to her place. This happened a few times. Each time the man placed his notes for the girl to take, he would look at Guru Dutt, as if challenging him to match his generosity.

Guru Dutt was quiet. I told him softly, 'Get some money out, we are being insulted.' But Guru Dutt did not pay any heed to me. The man now proceeded to place the money in front of Guru Dutt. The girl came around, offered the paan and her adaabs, and took the money. Still Guru Dutt did nothing. He took no notice of the man's insult. Emboldened by the silence, the man now took a ten-rupee note, circled it around Guru Dutt's head and placed it for the girl to pick it up. All through this, the singer watched and then fell silent.

The man now demanded ghungroos. 'I want you to dance,' he told the singer. She had been sitting all this while, her ghagra spread around her, her veil around her body. She now resisted having to dance, and demurred. But he was adamant. She finally put on the ghungroos offered to her and stood up to dance.

We were flabbergasted by what we saw. The girl was at least seven months' pregnant . . . and was preparing to dance for this lecherous man who sat alongside us. Guru Dutt got up. 'Let us go,' he said, and placing a thick roll of notes that must have been at least a thousand rupees, turned and left. We followed, sick in our hearts.

Guru Dutt was very angry. 'What sort of people would make a girl dance in her advanced state of pregnancy?' he ranted. I, for a change, said nothing . . . my mind was working. Later that evening, as we sat around drinking and eating, I could not get the sick feeling out of my mind and heart. Manu Bhai kept asking me to join the feast, but I was preoccupied. I kept saying, 'Later.'

Suddenly it hit me. I said, 'I have it.'

'What?' they chorused.

I turned to Guru Dutt, for he alone would know what I was talking about. 'I have the scene for Sahir's chakla,' I said. 'The hero will see a scene like the one we saw at the kotha, and he will leave in repulsion and then sing the chakla "*Jinhe naaz hai Hind par woh kahan hain* . . ."'

It was perhaps this that tilted the balance in Guru Dutt's mind in favour of seriously pursuing *Pyaasa*—the way the scene I had described fit the song he desperately wanted to immortalize on film.

We returned from Hyderabad determined to start the project in all earnestness, and the first scene we shot on our return to Bombay was the kotha scene and the song. However, Guru Dutt had to change the content of the scene in the interest of aesthetics. We could not have a heavily pregnant woman on screen, so we transformed the dancer into a mother of a sick baby and had the man make her dance even as the baby cried for her. It was poignant enough to sicken the hero's heart and make him turn away and leave the kotha, singing the powerful plaint by Sahir Ludhianvi that condemns the callousness of humanity.

Those days, I would go home with Guru Dutt every evening, and we would sit around with a drink each, discussing work. We started with *CID*, then the story and picturization of *Pyaasa* took over our lives. I was still a bachelor. It was in those long, fruitful evenings that I learnt a lot about Guru Dutt's technique and cinematic expression. I also learnt to drink. However, we never got really drunk, nor spent the time gossiping or maligning anybody.

Most of the time was spent talking films. He was a man obsessed with cinema.

✌

Till they decided to go full steam ahead with *Pyaasa*, only a few random outdoor scenes had been shot. Guru Dutt had cast Minoo Mumtaz to play the streetwalker's friend. Johnny Walker, now a constant in Guru Dutt Films, and a close friend of the director's, was signed to play the role of the friend who gives the poet shelter when he is homeless and later betrays him.

Abrar terms Guru Dutt's film-making technique as 'whimsical and unusual'. He would shoot scenes in any random order as the story developed. In fact, barring one or two exceptions, no Guru Dutt film was shot with a complete script in hand. 'The shooting would begin and we would expect the climax to resolve itself,' Abrar says.

Thus, it is to the director's credit that he managed to make not just coherent films but films that have stubbornly withstood the test of time. And his ear for music and eye for picturization have kept alive his song sequences so that they not only play on most 'old gold' channels on television and radio, but are also grist for the remix machine.

Elaborating on his director's mode of work, Abrar says that to Guru Dutt also goes the credit of shooting much more than needed: 'The raw stock he used for any one film could have finished three films.'

The 'history' of *Pyaasa* vindicates Abrar's statement.

By the time the film was actually ready, Guru Dutt had scrapped Minoo Mumtaz from the film. Her role went to Kumkum, who was given the song '*Jaane kya tune kahi*'. But in the final version of the film, it is Waheeda who sings the song. Similarly, Johnny Walker's scenes were shot, till, as the script progressed,

Guru Dutt felt that he did not want the comedian to play a negative role. The role of the hero's fickle friend was given to the actor Shyam. And Johnny Walker ended up immortalizing the character of the *maalishwala*. Abrar tells the story of how the role came about and the hit song that ended up on everyone's lips after Johnny Walker 'sang' it to entice his customers to subject themselves to his ministrations.

∽

I was asked to write a role for Johnny Walker, and it had to be a comic role. It was a last-minute order, and I had to find ways of fitting him in. Luckily for me, Guru Dutt himself solved my problem.

The unit was in Calcutta, searching for suitable locations, and Guru Dutt was quite taken by two aspects of a city he loved. The *phuchkas* (as *pani puris* are called in Calcutta) and the spicy puffed rice or *jhal muri* were favourites and he would eat them sitting on the lawns of Victoria Memorial.

It was on one such occasion that Guru Dutt chanced to see a maalishwala. The checked lungi, the jaunty cap and baniyan, the paraphernalia of glass bottles of oil . . . all of it seemed so right for the characterization. And so the role came to life.

As did the song '*Sar jo tera chakraye*'. Guru Dutt had picked up a bunch of 78 rpm records of English songs during his visit to England. There was one tune he liked a lot, and he decided to graft it on to *Pyaasa*. It was from the film *Harry Black and the Tiger*, which, though Guru Dutt did not know it then, would be released later in India. S.D. Burman, who was composing the music for the film, was asked to copy the song note for note. Of course, Dada Burman was very upset by the instruction. He came to me and said, 'What is this that Guru is asking of me, *public mujhe marega*. Please explain to him, he listens to you, let me put in a little of my own tune into the song . . . change it a bit . . .'

But Guru Dutt was adamant—the tune would have to be copied hundred per cent in the *mukhda* at least. 'Let him do what he wants in the *antara*,' he decreed and Burman Dada had to be content with that.

❧

However, the music director waved his baton effectively enough to blend the tune with his own melody in such a manner that no one really noticed the surgery, and the song remains a hit even today. 'In fact, later, when the producer of *Harry Black and the Tiger* visited India, he heard the song and not only failed to recognize the tune, but commended Dada on it,' Abrar laughs.

Johnny Walker's role as Kumkum's sweetheart, who is also the common point of contact for Waheeda the streetwalker and Guru Dutt the poet, remains one of the most memorable ones in his long career.

The songs of *Pyaasa* are eternal favourites with music lovers. And they range in style from the poignant 'chakla' by Sahir that Guru Dutt plucked out of his collection to immortalize in the film, to the dream sequence orchestrated between Guru Dutt, the impoverished student–poet, and his rich sweetheart, played by Mala Sinha.

Guru Dutt revelled in his love for song picturization, and it is to his credit and to that of his contemporary, Raj Kapoor, that while they brought in an element of the fabulous into the visualization of songs, they also ensured that the song served a specific narrative purpose. Thus, in the dream sequence, the opulent, surreal set which served as a backdrop for the waltzy song-and-dance number does not exist in a vacuum—it shows up the disparity in backgrounds between the lovers.

Abrar has other stories about the songs of *Pyaasa*. As far as the chronology of song recordings went, the third song to be recorded after the 'chakla' and '*Sar jo tera*' was '*Jaane woh kaise log the*'. Also written by Sahir, the song was a plaint by the poet, who is indirectly telling the woman who had been his beloved in college that he is hurt by the way she has rejected him for the comfort of being a rich man's wife. But, Abrar begins with what he considers the most interesting of the 'song stories'—the recording of a song by Mohammad Rafi.

∽

The lyrics of '*Tung aa chuke hain kashmakash-e-zindagi se hum*', the nazm the poet sings at his college reunion (and incidentally hears the streetwalker humming when he sees her the first time), have a deep, abiding pathos. Guru Dutt and I discussed thoroughly how the two college lovers of *Pyaasa* would meet again. I said, 'They met over poetry the first time, let there be a scene that unites them again over poetry, so that poetry is the leitmotif of their relationship.' Guru Dutt agreed it was fitting.

It was decided that a poem by Sahir should be used for the scene. Burman Dada had to work out a tune for the poem. On the appointed date, Rafi, who was a thorough professional, came over to Guru Dutt's place for the sitting right on time. But unfortunately for us, Dada was nowhere to be seen. I told Rafi, 'You are a master at music, why don't you recite the poem in your own style?'

Rafi thought about it a bit, and then started reciting the poem in the clear, musical voice that was his signature. And we recorded it right there, on a spool of tape, on Guru Dutt's tape recorder. So clear and distinct was the voice and the recording that we could use the copy as it was without having to record it again in a studio. In fact, the somewhat rough quality of the recording gave the scene greater authenticity.

Coming to '*Jaane woh kaise log the*', the tune of the song was inspired by a Rabindranath Tagore composition and it was Rafi who was to sing it as he was singing the other songs for the hero. However, one evening, we were driving somewhere. I remember I was in the front seat, next to the driver, and Guru Dutt and wife Geeta were in the back.

I suggested to him that the song might sound better in Hemant Kumar's voice. Guru Dutt was aghast. 'Are you mad?' he asked. 'How can a man sing in two voices in one film? Rafi is the voice we have already used for him. Anyway, Rafi is not a bad singer . . .'

He turned to Geeta and asked her for her opinion. Surprisingly, Geeta went with my idea. 'Hemant has a low bass voice which will suit the song better,' she opined. Guru Dutt was silent for a moment and did not comment. I do not know how far Geeta's opinion influenced his decision, but as we all know, Hemant Kumar sang that song.

❧

Then there is the remarkable tale about the song that *Pyaasa* is most remembered for: the film's unforgettable climax in which, at the death anniversary of the poet–hero, his publisher is holding a commemorative function in his memory. Abrar has his own way of telling the story that is still fresh in his memory.

❧

I had gone away for some weeks for an operation, which had almost turned into an emergency. In the meantime, Guru Dutt remained busy with *Pyaasa* and continued with his shooting schedule.

We had worked out the details of the scene where Guru Dutt returns to be present at his own death anniversary function. I had yet to write the dialogues, but I told Guru Dutt, let's get the song ready, and I will write the dialogues when I return.

Sahir Ludhianvi, who had written all the other songs, wrote this one too. But somewhere along the way, he seemed to have lost track of the milieu of the story. However, the song he wrote had enough punch and pathos in it to excite the director in Guru Dutt, who filmed it immediately.

I returned to the sets, fresh from my convalescence and Guru Dutt triumphantly showed me the rushes of the song. I was impressed by the wonderful way he had shot it, but the lyrics dismayed me. Guru Dutt could not understand why, so I had to explain. 'The era we have placed the film in is the mid-fifties,' I said, 'and Sahir has written about the *mahelon*, the *takhton*, the *tajon ki duniya* . . . these symbols of the Raj, royalty and the zamindari are defunct; that era is past in the period our movie is set in, we are a democratic nation. So what *duniya* are we referring to?'

Of course, it was impossible to change the lyrics; the song had already been shot. I had to do some damage control at my end and bring relevance to the lines if we were not to seem anachronistic and foolishly out of date. I thought about it seriously and decided to give Rehman, the publisher, some rhetoric that would justify the references to royalty. Which is why Rehman talks about the dead poet and says that if Vijay were alive today he would place him on a takht and place a crown (taj) on his head . . . which Vijay, standing framed in a flood of light at the door of the hall, overhears and responds to with the now-famous renunciation of the world of falsehood and hypocrisy.

12

Bade Dhoke Hain Is Raah Mein

Abrar did not know it while he was writing *Pyaasa*, but the film was to give him his first taste of direction too. It happened without warning.

⌒

Like I usually did every day, I ambled in to the sets of *Pyaasa* at leisure, in time to give the artists their dialogues. The schedule normally started at nine-thirty in the morning, but I knew that lighting would take time, and the make-up too, and so I would go in when I knew I could start work.

The set for *Pyaasa* was in Famous Studio, on the ground floor. Guru Dutt's office was on the first floor. We were shooting a street scene that day. A taxi drives up and comes to a halt. A girl is thrown out of the taxi. The cab door is closed by a hand from the inside, and the girl leaps up, grabs the hand and demands her money. From inside the taxi, the man, whose face is still in shadow, says, '*Chal hatt,*' and the taxi drives away. The girl, stunned and disbelieving, turns to see a policeman watching her rather suspiciously. She starts to walk away. The policeman follows her. She starts running. The girl then turns into a narrow gully, where the hero is seen approaching. He gauges the situation. After a few hurried dialogues, when the policeman nears her, the hero holds the girl in his arms and she hides her face in his chest. When the policeman sees them and confronts him, the hero tells him that the girl is his wife. The policeman moves away and the hero tells the girl she can go safely now, but she turns to him with a strange look on her face. The hero moves away and climbs the stairs nearby which lead to a terrace. He stands there with his back to the stairs, smoking. The girl climbs the stairs behind him, moves, as if she wants to cling to him, hesitates, and the song by the devdasi on the street begins: '*Aaj sajan mohe ang laga lo . . .*'

There were only one or two lines of dialogue so I expected a cool, laidback morning. I couldn't have been more mistaken. I was given no time. I must have walked in at about ten, and everyone was lolling around . . . the lights were not up, there was no sign that the shift had begun.

'What happened?' I asked.

'We were waiting for you,' they answered. 'Guru Dutt has decided that you will shoot today.'

I said, 'Where is Guru Dutt? Let me sort it out with him.' I sought him out, asked him for an explanation. He said, 'You will have to shoot, as we cannot waste the day. I have to go attend to a court case.'

I protested. I had never wielded the director's megaphone before, but he was firm and insistent. 'Shoot just what you have written,' he said. 'After all, you wrote it, and so must have visualized it too. Shoot it your way. Tell Murthy to light the shot the way you want it.'

'What if I make a mistake?' I countered.

He brushed off my hesitation. 'We'll just shoot it again,' he said. 'Anyway, the rushes will be in tomorrow.'

I went to the set. I asked Murthy, Guru Dutt's cinematographer, for feedback, but he would not volunteer anything. I was forced to think things out for myself. I began to work the scene out and we started shooting.

❧

It was only much later, when his job was almost done, that Abrar discovered that he had been the victim of an elaborate set-up. And found the real reason for Murthy's uncooperative attitude. Abrar laughs at the memory. Murthy had been well tutored. Sometime in the afternoon, Abrar noticed that the cameraman kept glancing upwards. The scene was almost done by then and Abrar was less preoccupied with it and began to notice things around him. It struck him that Murthy was looking up once too often for no apparent reason. He followed Murthy's gaze and saw, high on the second floor, Guru Dutt standing, leaning forward, his elbows resting against the banister, watching everything happening on the set below. He must have watched the entire scene being set up and shot. It was only then that Abrar realized that the director was testing his writer.

Guru Dutt had a reason for the test. Later, he would ask Abrar to direct a film. For the time being, however, it was clear to Abrar that he had passed the directorial test. 'Nothing in the scene I had shot was changed. It went to the screen in exactly the way I had shot it.'

Though he found enough potential in Abrar Alvi to see him in the image of a director, even before Abrar saw himself in the role, the hold Guru Dutt had on his medium was tenacious and focused. 'Though I was the writer, it was he as director who set the tone for *Pyaasa*,' Abrar says.

Especially in the characterization of the streetwalker.

❧

I wanted to be realistic. I wanted Waheeda to speak as Gulabo had done in real life—her language needed to be harsh. I wanted her to move in a certain way. Guru Dutt had never met the original Gulabo. He had only my word sketch of her to go by, and his own sensibilities coloured his characterization of Gulabo on screen.

We had a number of arguments and discussions on the subject, but his will prevailed. My creative grouse was that she came across as too nice to be a streetwalker. Which prostitute reads poetry, is a connoisseur of literature? I felt his characterization was preposterous. But maybe the sort of character I had in mind would not have suited Waheeda. I had even given Waheeda a cigarette; it was taken away in a huff. However, now I do believe that Guru Dutt was right, because Gulabo as a character in *Pyaasa* has become a part of film history.

Meanwhile, Guru Dutt kept bringing up the topic of Abrar directing a film under his banner. He had a story, *Bachelor Mother*, a Ginger Rogers film which he felt could be adapted in Hindi. Abrar was asked to rehash the script, and he did adapt and rewrite it for Indian audiences. Once the script was ready, Guru Dutt asked Abrar to launch it as his directorial venture.

We were almost done with *Pyaasa*. One evening, we were just sitting around at the studio. The mood was upbeat. *CID* had been doing wonderfully well, and was on its way to its silver jubilee week at the Minerva Theatre in Bombay. And *Pyaasa* too seemed to have turned out satisfactorily. One thing led to another, and while we were talking of many things, Guru Dutt started again on the topic of my turning director under his banner.

'I keep telling Abrar to direct, but he won't listen,' he said. 'He does not realize he is so lucky. In my time, we used to go to Mukherjee, the producer, with a file under the arm and beg to be given a chance to direct.'

I, of course, had to reply to that. I told him, 'There is a difference. Being an assistant director is not a career, it's only a stepping stone to a career. So every assistant director needs to become a director to find his place in the sun. Being a writer, however, is a full-fledged career. I am a writer, and I want to attain the greatest heights I can as a writer. After that, direction will come to me on its own. If Rajinder Krishan wants to become a director, he can do so tomorrow, because he has reached that stage. I too want to get there. You were then seeking a career . . . I already have mine.'

At this point, I remember Raj Khosla turning to Guru Dutt. 'If Abrar does not want to direct the film, let him be,' he said, 'don't worry about him. Give me the film and I will direct it.'

I was also in high spirits, having drunk as much as any of them. I rose to the challenge. 'The day I decide to direct a film in this concern, under this banner,' I told Raj, 'you will stand no chance against me.'

Raj Khosla was basking in the glory of having directed a super hit in *CID*. Turning to Guru Dutt, he asked plaintively, 'Is that true? Will he be a better director than I am? Is he better than me?'

Guru Dutt, of course, kept his counsel. He only smiled. We were like his pet *murgas*, fighter cocks. He quite enjoyed pitting one against another, me against Raj, or against Johnny Walker, and sitting back and listening to us bicker. But at the bottom of all that, we were all pretty close to one another.

But, coming back to the adaptation of *Bachelor Mother*, I was not inspired by the story. I believed that the basic premise of the film was wrong. How could a woman not recognize a man who is wooing her, and whom she loves, just because he is wearing false whiskers and a false beard? Also, I was very caught up with *Pyaasa*, which was occupying all my creative energies. And so I passed up the chance to direct the new film.

෴

The film was later made as *Professor*. And it ran a chequered course before it actually went into production.

Angry and upset after discovering that Abrar was writing for another producer without informing him, Guru Dutt, during the last days of *Pyaasa*'s shooting, almost fired his writer and chief assistant. The incident had Guru Dutt stomping off to his office and getting his typist to pound out a letter terminating Abrar's services. The exact words, as Abrar recollects, were: 'Your services are no longer required by Guru Dutt Films, forthwith.'

Almost at the same time a second letter was also dictated in which the direction of *Professor* was handed over to one Shashi Bhushan, who had earlier approached Guru Dutt to give him a film to direct. When the tensions between Guru Dutt and Abrar Alvi reached a fever pitch over the latter's writing for another producer, Guru Dutt gave *Professor* to Shashi Bhushan who was conveniently around.

Unaware of the storm brewing on the sets of *Pyaasa*, when Abrar, who had been playing truant on the particular day he had been caught out, reported on the sets the next day, a surprise awaited him. He was to give the dialogues for the final scene and Guru Dutt was engrossed with a shot. But as he pulled out the sheet with the dialogues from his pocket, as was his habit, another sheet of paper was thrust into his hand by Guruswamy.

He could not believe his eyes. He read the letter, then told Guruswamy, 'But the last scene has to be shot, I have brought it along. Ask Guru Dutt if he wants the scene. If he does, I shall leave it behind, if he doesn't, I can take it back with me.'

Dutifully, Guruswamy returned to the sets to ask Guru Dutt about the dialogues. He came back to ask Abrar to wait. 'He'll come soon,' he added. Abrar, with all the petulance of a whipped child, sat outside, while Guru Dutt finished the song he was shooting. In a while the director came out to meet Abrar. Johnny Walker was also with him.

❧

They were both smiling at me, but Guru Dutt asked me sarcastically, 'So you have come, you have finally found the time to do so!'

I held up the letter I had been given. 'I have got this love letter,' I said.

Guru Dutt asked me why, instead of sneaking off to freelance behind his back, I had not asked for more money.

'Am I a beggar?' I retorted. 'You should understand . . . a man's needs grow.'

By that time, Guru Dutt's anger had cooled. He reached across, took the letter from me and tore it up. It was a two-hour notice . . . I was back in service.

❧

But the letter given to Shashi Bhushan was quite another matter. 'The story and script were mine,' says Abrar, 'the title had been given by Guru Dutt, and Shashi Bhushan's contribution to the entire project was almost nil. Guru Dutt himself decided to drop the project.'

Shashi, however, took the script to F.C. Mehra of Eagle Films, who liked it and cast Shammi Kapoor in it. Shammi Kapoor was a close friend of Lekh Tandon, who had been a co-assistant with Abrar under C.L. Dheer. In fact, Lekh Tandon's father knew the

Kapoor family very well, and when Lekh first came down to Bombay to work in films, he had stayed with Raj Kapoor. He called Krishna Kapoor 'bhabhi'. Though he was older than Shammi Kapoor, he was closer to Shammi than to Raj.

Shammi Kapoor had started his career with small roles, and had found his métier with Nasir Hussain's comedies, starting with *Tumsa Nahin Dekha*. But as luck would have it, some tension had developed between the actor and his favourite producer–director and Shammi was looking for a new partner.

He had heard of Abrar's skill in writing modern comedies that had contemporary language and had approached him to write for his next venture. The film titled *Mujrim* was to be produced by F.C. Mehra.

'I did not know who the producer was, and had not heard of the director either, and knowing that it was not reason enough to seek Guru Dutt's permission to write for a banner other than his own, I turned down the offer,' Abrar says.

But as things went, Lekh Tandon managed to get Shammi to agree to give him the direction of *Professor*, his next film. Of course, Shammi had his own condition. He wanted Abrar to write the film for him and producer F.C. Mehra.

So Abrar ended up writing the dialogues and screenplay for *Professor*. The writing done, this time with Guru Dutt's blessings and permission, 'for Lekh's sake', Abrar returned to his work with Guru Dutt Films.

But the *Professor* saga wasn't over yet.

'One day, Lekh came running to me,' Abrar continues. Lekh felt Shammi wanted to return to Nasir Hussain. '*Mera patta kat gaya*,' he cried and beseeched Abrar to help him.

That was when Abrar decided to draw up a contract with Mehra.

❧

I went to him and said I wanted a contract stating that I had done the script, dialogues and screenplay for the film, and that the direction would be given to Lekh Tandon. Mehra was surprised. 'The contract is between me and you, why should Lekh's name feature in it?' he asked.

You see I had accepted a ridiculously low amount for writing *Professor*. I had already been talking to Tarachand Barjatya about writing for his banner and I had quoted a price of Rs 30,000 and finally agreed to Rs 25,000. But since Lekh was supposed to direct *Professor*, for his sake I agreed to reconsider my market rate and fixed the price at Rs 17,500.

I told Mehra that it was only because of Lekh that I had written the film for such a low price, less than half my market rate . . . and if he did not give Lekh the direction, I would take the script and screenplay and give it to someone else. After all, there was nothing in writing to say I was contracted to give it to Eagle Films. And that is how Lekh got to direct *Professor*.

Guru Dutt debuted as director with *Baazi* (1951, left) and followed it up with *Jaal* (1952, centre right), both classic Hindi film noirs. Abrar came to the Guru Dutt fold when the latter was making *Baaz* (1953, top left). But his work on the film, one he describes as 'a mad idea…a crazy drama on the high seas', was limited to driving the film's side hero (his cousin) to the sets and its producer on her shopping sprees.

Guru Dutt productions'
AAR-PAAR
Directed by GURU DUTT Music O.P. NAYYAR

With *Aar Paar* (1954), Guru Dutt established his own production house, Guru Dutt Films. The film, which marked the beginning of the collaboration between Guru Dutt and Abrar Alvi, became a trendsetter in Hindi cinema with its natural everyday dialogues.

Based on a play, *A Modern Marriage*, that Abrar had written during his college days, *Mr and Mrs '55* (1955) was Guru Dutt's only foray into comic territory and introduced Madhubala as an actress capable of handling comedy.

Abrar Alvi's chance meeting with a prostitute was the genesis of the character of Gulabo in *Pyaasa* (1957), immortalized on screen by Waheeda Rehman in her first major Hindi film role. The relationship between the angst-ridden poet and the prostitute who adores his poetry was loosely based on Abrar's relationship with the real-life Gulabo.

Now considered a masterpiece, *Kaagaz Ke Phool* (1959) was a commercial and critical failure at the time. It boasted of technical experiments in lighting and framing never attempted before in Indian cinema. While Guru Dutt admitted that the movie 'went over the heads' of his audience, Abrar believes that it didn't do well because audiences could not identify with the mental angst of a well-to-do man unhappy over his lack of intellectual and creative freedom.

A stylish thriller, *CID* introduced Waheeda Rehman to Hindi cinema as a vamp with a golden heart. Its memorable climax was scripted by Abrar who was not formally associated with the film.

Chaudhvin Ka Chand (1960) was based on a story and script by Shaukat Rizvi, which Abrar disliked and disagreed with. Though not formally associated with the film, he reworked Rizvi's story 'Ek Jhalak' into *Chaudhvin Ka Chand*, Guru Dutt's most successful film till *Sahib Bibi Aur Ghulam*.

According to Abrar, 'Guru Dutt wanted Chhoti Bahu to look wanton and motherly and beseeching.' Meena Kumari fit the bill and under Abrar's direction she came up with the finest performance of her career.

Even forty-five years after its release, the view persists that Abrar Alvi was only a front for Guru Dutt who actually directed *Sahib Bibi Aur Ghulam*. Abrar sets the record straight with his account of the making of a veritable classic of Indian cinema.

Abrar Alvi with Guru Dutt at the premiere of *Pyaasa* (1957).

Abrar Alvi (facing camera) directing on the sets of *Sahib Bibi Aur Ghulam*.

Abrar Alvi (extreme right) with Guru Dutt and Waheeda Rehman at the Berlin Film Festival in 1963.

13

Kisko Fursat Hai Jo Thaame
Diwanon Ka Haath

The film that is today considered Guru Dutt's greatest work might have been very different if he had succeeded in executing his idea of casting someone other than himself as the hero. The actor he wanted to cast was Dilip Kumar, then at the height of his career, an established star, and an actor whose prowess in performing any role, however demanding, had been proved beyond doubt.

A few reels of *Pyaasa* had already been shot. Waheeda was well into her groove with the dance number in *CID*, 'Kahin pe nigahen ...' and was waiting to sink her teeth into the characterization of the streetwalker in *Pyaasa*, which was slowly turning into quite a serious film. When Guru Dutt, who had no illusions about his acting skills and in fact underestimated himself considerably as an actor, realized where *Pyaasa* was heading in terms of tone, he decided that a more skilled actor should wear the hero's mantle. He still wanted to direct the film, and felt all the more that his attention would be diverted by the dual responsibility. He broached the subject with Abrar.

∽

'Let us scrap what has been shot with me, and let us cast Dilip Kumar in my role,' he said to me one day.

By then I was close enough to him to be able to make suggestions. I said, 'Let us give Dilip saab a narration.' It was agreed that Guru Dutt and I would sit for a session with the actor. My memory power was great those days and I could recite whole portions of the script almost verbatim. The story session went on till almost two-thirty in the morning, with discussions on who else could be cast in the film.

Dilip Kumar had strong views on the role of the streetwalker. He said, 'The streetwalker cannot be the heroine of the film.' Of course, there was a reason for this. He wanted Madhubala to play the heroine. I fought the issue out. I told Dilip Kumar that such a change was not possible.

'You are a fine writer,' Dilip Kumar insisted. 'If you put your mind to it, it can be done.'

I said, 'Of course I can, but it will be another film altogether.'

Ultimately, Dilip Kumar gave up. All through our discussions and arguments, Guru Dutt was a silent spectator.

❧

The real reason for Dilip Kumar's desire to change the focus from the streetwalker was that Madhubala wanted to play the role that was eventually essayed by Mala Sinha. So, Dilip Kumar kept insisting that some twist be given to the story to make the hero's college sweetheart's role a sympathetic one, while the streetwalker should become a shadowy character in the film. But finally, Abrar convinced him, and Dilip Kumar said, 'Okay, I'll go with it, let me see how you take it forward.'

❧

At that point, as it was quite late in the night and we were all exhausted, Guru Dutt said, 'Right, we shall talk money in the morning.'

The next day we went across to the star. Dilip Kumar quoted his going rate of one-and-a-half lakh. Guru Dutt asked him to consider cutting his price. 'I need to scrap the three reels I have shot that have me playing the role,' he said.

To that, Dilip Kumar said, 'You needn't worry. You will get your price from the market. I have fixed distributors and they will cover your money.'

Guru Dutt told him, 'I have fixed distributors too and they have been taking all my pictures. I have already worked out my deal with them . . . I cannot change them as I am already committed.'

'Tell them you have signed on Dilip Kumar, they will automatically raise their price.'

Guru Dutt would have none of it. 'I have already committed to them,' he said, 'and they have taken it on trust with no conditions. By taking you I cannot raise the price, it would be unethical. I haven't come to you to sell my film. I can sell it on my own. I have come to you as a director, because I believe that if I cast you in my film, I will make a better film. You will add stature to it.'

Dilip Kumar took umbrage at the statement. Later on, his sycophants and advisors had long arguments with Abrar on what Guru Dutt had really meant. But that day the thespian simply said, 'Fine, we shall shoot from tomorrow.' The next day, the entire unit of *Pyaasa*, along with its director and writer, waited four hours for the new star of the film to make his appearance. Guruswamy and Abrar went to a Bengali gentleman at Bombay Talkies who was a friend of Dilip Kumar, but he had no idea where the actor was.

❧

We made many phone calls to Dilip Kumar's residence, but there was no sign of him. Those days, artists were not in the habit of coming in as late as they do nowadays, so it was really unusual. There was no trace of the man. At four p.m. I told Guru Dutt to put on his make-up and start the shift. We had waited long enough believing Dilip Kumar would come. Till today, we do not know why he did not turn up after promising to do so. And so the shooting resumed with Guru Dutt in the lead role.

❧

Pyaasa gave comedian Mehmood his first break in Guru Dutt Films. Another comedian, Johnny Walker, introduced Mehmood to Guru Dutt and suggested he be given a role. Guru Dutt obliged his friend by asking Abrar to write in a role for the young newcomer. 'I just added a brother to Guru Dutt's family in *Pyaasa*, and Mehmood stepped into the film,' Abrar says. As *CID* was also being made at the same time, Mehmood was given the role of a gangster in that film; the script demanded that a gangster be killed in lock-up, and Mehmood was asked to play the part.

Mehmood and his sister, Minoo Mumtaz, had been performing artists since they were practically children. Minoo would dance and Mehmood would do a series of funny acts and some mimicry and singing. Now, working with the Guru Dutt Films banner, a new world opened up for Mehmood. As the films progressed and Mehmood worked on his roles, he soaked in the sense of camaraderie that existed in the Guru Dutt Films unit. Along the way, he realized that a few people in the unit were part of Guru Dutt's coterie. He wanted to be a part of this inner circle.

❧

At that time, when we were making *CID* and *Pyaasa*, most of the unit was under thirty years of age. I was twenty-six when *Pyaasa* was completed in 1956; Guru Dutt was about twenty-eight. His good looks, his expertise and exquisite craftsmanship had already earned him a reputation and there was an aura of glamour attached to him that reflected on his company too. Mehmood would often ask me what he could do to be part of the charmed inner circle. To his credit, Mehmood had an innate ability to entertain us all. He was always ready with jokes and puns; he would mimic others and could easily make us laugh. There were times when he would pit his wits against Johnny Walker, only to realize that he had more than met his match, but he was sporting enough not to let that upset him.

Realizing I was close to Guru Dutt, Mehmood got after me. 'Abrar Bhai,' he would say, 'I want to get close to Guru Dutt, he respects you, do something for me . . .' We were all on location in Calcutta, and I conveyed his wish to Guru Dutt. Of course he was amused, but he said nothing. In his characteristic manner, he filed away the information to use later. One evening, we were all sitting together over drinks. Guru Dutt, his assistant Niranjan, and a few others were present, and so was I. Guru Dutt decided to have some fun.

Guru Dutt knew Mehmood did not drink, yet he sent for him. When Mehmood arrived, Guru Dutt made him repeat his pledge that he would do 'anything' to be allowed into the inner circle. Mehmood solemnly stated that he was prepared to do anything. Guru Dutt then asked him to have a drink; after all he had to be able to sit and drink with the group if he wanted to be part of it. Mehmood refused. At that point, everyone went after him, reminding him he had pledged to do 'anything'.

'If you refuse to drink, we will have to force it down your throat,' someone said, and the mood got boisterous. We caught him and pinned him down. All through the scuffle, Mehmood kept saying, 'Please don't, let me go.' When a glass of liquor was brought to his lips, he shook his head violently and clenched his teeth, ensuring that none of the liquid passed his lips or entered his throat. And when he could speak, he begged us to let him go.

Guru Dutt watched this from his seat and finally told us to lay off. He realized that Mehmood was serious about not drinking and was not just shamming modesty. He said quietly, '*Bas karo, bahut ho gaya.*'

We remonstrated with Mehmood. Asked him what he had against drinking. Look at us, we said, we drink so often, has the liquor turned us into bad men, or monsters? Are we misbehaving? Have we become demonic? Why are you making such a fuss?

He looked at us and said, 'My father drank so much alcohol in his lifetime that for many generations his progeny will have traces of liquor in their veins.'

It was indeed a sobering moment.

Mehmood told them how his father, Mumtaz Ali, had succumbed to alcohol. Mumtaz Ali, along with Cuckoo, had been a star in his own right. A famous dancer, he had held the same status in the film industry as any lead actor and had shared top billing in many films. In fact, the film *Basant* (1942) had a dance number every ten or twelve minutes to showcase his dances, and drew immense crowds to each show.

But when Mumtaz Ali started to lose his sense of discipline thanks to alcohol, he stopped getting offers. Slowly he began to run out of work. Because he had a sizeable fan following, a tour was organized for him across many cities and towns in India. A series of theatres were booked for his performances, and tickets sold briskly. At the first of these shows, as the audience thronged the theatre and the curtain went up, a crisis erupted backstage. Mumtaz Ali's name was announced repeatedly, but instead of taking the stage the dancer was lying in a drunken stupor in the wings.

To pacify the irate, impatient audience that demanded its money back and seemed angry enough to burn down the theatre, the organizer sent Minoo Mumtaz and Mehmood onstage, introducing them as the children of Mumtaz Ali who would perform a couple of opening numbers before the maestro came on.

That was how Mehmood was launched as a performing artist. Mumtaz Ali lost everything he had earned to drink. His property disappeared, dissolved in bottles of liquor; he found himself deeply in debt and virtually penniless. And that, Mehmood said, was why he had sworn off drink.

Of course, Guru Dutt respected that sentiment. But he was never above a bit of mischievous fun, and quite often Mehmood was an easy target. Abrar narrates another incident.

One day when I walked into the office, Guru Dutt called out to me. 'Come, we will have some fun,' he said. I wondered what mischief he had thought up this time and waited to find out. Shyam Kapoor, another assistant, who had obviously been given due instructions, walked up casually to Mehmood and touched his nose. Before Mehmood could retaliate, he ran away.

Mehmood reacted in an amazing manner. He shouted loudly and took off after Shyam. Mehmood was superstitious about someone touching his nose—he believed it would bring him bad luck. The only way he could ward off the evil effects that seemed imminent was to touch Shyam Kapoor's nose in return.

But Shyam seemed to have disappeared. Mehmood turned to Guru Dutt and said, 'Dada, call him.' He sat, looking very disturbed, and one of the others took him out supposedly to search for Shyam, who, of course, was nearby and let himself be 'spotted'.

Mehmood lunged after him and there ensued a merry chase. The studio had lush gardens and a waterfall and we watched with growing merriment as a distraught Mehmood chased Shyam around the entire area. Finally, half an hour later, Guru Dutt called out to Shyam and he let Mehmood touch his nose.

～

Mehmood, like Johnny Walker, became a permanent fixture in Guru Dutt Films. In *Kaagaz Ke Phool*, he was given a few lines to mouth in a picnic song sequence. Though the roles were almost inconsequential, Mehmood insisted on taking them on just to be part of the ventures. He needed to be in every Guru Dutt film, even if it was only in an extra's role, and even if he had other films in hand.

This professional association ended with *Sahib Bibi Aur Ghulam* in which Mehmood had no role. Neither did Johnny Walker. As Abrar explains, neither comedian fitted into the setting of the film. And Abrar did not want to cast either of them. He believed that he had already erred once in casting Johnny Walker in *Kaagaz Ke Phool*. He was unwilling to repeat the mistake. Besides, as he says, he did not want to 'mess around with a novel'. Guru Dutt's commitment notwithstanding, there would be no role for either comedian in *Sahib Bibi Aur Ghulam*.

～

I had made a mistake in giving Johnny Walker the role of a westernized, Anglicized gentleman in *Kaagaz Ke Phool*. It was beyond him. He was wonderfully cut out for roles that had a local trait which he could adopt but he was woefully out of his depth in *Kaagaz*. For one, he had trouble pronouncing English words at that time. He would say 'k-lub' instead of club, irrespective of the number of times we rehearsed him. But the casting was done and we had to live with it. Guru Dutt was a bit unhappy with my decision not to take him in *Sahib Bibi Aur Ghulam*. He had always had a role marked out for Johnny Walker in every film to date, because he felt that not taking him would disappoint his friend. I assured him I would talk to Johnny and explain things to him.

❦

Abrar met Johnny Walker and fleshed out the entire setting and the period mood of *Sahib Bibi Aur Ghulam* to him. He delineated the main roles in the film and asked Johnny whether he felt any of them was right for him. Johnny Walker was discerning enough to perceive that he did not see a role for himself in the film and was magnanimous enough to accept that without rancour.

In fact, the friendship between Abrar Alvi and Johnny Walker burned with a steady flame over the years. Johnny Walker lived close to Abrar's house and the writer visited the comedian every week, to spend a few hours talking of old times. It was when Johnny Walker died that the real extent of Abrar's fondness for him became evident to me. He was pensive, his grief translating into a series of stories of their days together with Guru Dutt, the bond that cemented two very different personalities.

❦

We were very different from each other. Guru Dutt and I were both essentially loners. Johnny Walker, on the other hand, was comfortable in a crowd. But the difference in our temperaments never came in the way of our friendship. Johnny Walker's real name was Badruddin Qazi and I remember him as a funny, lively man. A great admirer of top Hindi comedian Charlie (Noor Mohammad, who took the screen name inspired by Chaplin), Johnny Walker used to copy his body language and mannerisms.

Johnny had been a bus conductor in Indore with dreams of becoming an actor. To prepare himself, he learned, of all things, stunt cycling. In *Baharen*, he has a scene where he jumps on to the handlebar of the heroine's bicycle. I used his agility with the bicycle to advantage. Before coming to Bombay, he had also been a vendor selling fruit ice cream on his bicycle between Nashik and Deolali. In Bombay, he found a perfect setting for himself at the Mahim mela. He would wear a clown's hat, give speeches to make people laugh, assume different personae, mimic various sales people. God had given him a unique gift: he could roll his tongue such that the tip would touch the back. It gave him, I think, amazing dexterity in expressing various sounds.

Before long he landed an extra's role and used it to get noticed. He had the extraordinary ability to keep everyone amused with his witticisms while never imposing himself. It must have been very helpful during the long hours of waiting that are part of an extra's life. It was Balraj Sahni who introduced Johnny to Guru Dutt. Johnny had shot a scene as an extra with Balraj Sahni in the Dilip Kumar film, *Hulchul*. Balraj, who was at the time scripting *Baazi* for Guru Dutt and Dev Anand, wrote in a small role for Johnny Walker in the film. The scene showed Dev Anand and Johnny Walker in jail. Johnny, being the man he was, improvised and ad-libbed brilliantly. Guru Dutt took a liking to the comedian and the foundation of a very sincere friendship was laid.

Though everyone in Guru Dutt Films was immensely fond of Guru Dutt, Johnny and I were really close to him. You could call us the three musketeers. As a writer and assistant director in charge of the actors, I was very strict about actors sticking to what I said and to the lines exactly as I had written them. I changed this rule only for Johnny Walker. He would add his own bits and get away with it. To be honest, his improvisations were always spot on. They never sounded wrong or out of place.

Both Johnny and Guru Dutt liked shikar. Guru Dutt would often call us out of the blue, 'Come, get ready, let's go' and we would drive off. It was Johnny who made Guru Dutt buy a rifle to go hunting. And it was thanks to Johnny that Guru Dutt started eating meat though his family was vegetarian. Both of them also loved to fly kites. Guru Dutt would tell me, 'Johnny is on the roof flying a kite, let's go.' I would reply that I was not fond of flying kites, but he would say, 'Come, let us at least sit together.' They would go fishing together and I would be roped in. I'd sit with them on their machans in Powai, overlooking the lake.

❧

The three musketeers enjoyed a unique professional and personal relationship. If Johnny Walker was not as close to Guru Dutt as Abrar was, it is because he was incredibly busy right through the 1950s. He was, after all, the top comedian of the era. He had a number of films on hand at any given time and seldom had time to listen to Guru Dutt when he was in one of his 'moods'. Abrar had both the time and the opportunity to get closer.

Among the many adventures the three of them had, Abrar mentions one where Guru Dutt tried his hand at being a part-time farmer and a brewer. Guru Dutt had a farm in Lonavala and was building a farmhouse on it. He bought a trailer with a bath and bedroom and a mechanical plough. He attached the trailer to his Plymouth but it was too heavy, so he got himself a jeep station wagon.

❧

'Get ready, we have to leave this evening for Lonavala,' Guru Dutt said over the phone one day. 'Pack enough clothes for two to three days.'

The three of us drove off at eight-thirty at night, the driver driving the jeep, we in the trailer. It was a very uncomfortable journey, with the trailer swinging and swerving all the way. Guru Dutt was full of plans about farming in his free time. We reached the farm at dawn. Guru Dutt had planned to live in the trailer but by midday we found it too hot to endure. So we had to hire a room for a day. One trip and he had had enough of farming. He gave the trailer away to Geeta Bali.

Once the farmhouse was built, we went across more often. Guru Dutt became friendly with some tribal people who lived nearby. He came to know that they made country liquor, and wanted to learn how to make some too. One evening, he decided to go to the farmhouse despite my remonstrations about it being too hot there. We drove up and I saw that his farmhouse had been converted into a brewery. A full scale 'operation liquor' was in progress, and he sat watching it, like a little boy watching a science experiment. Then, turning down the Scotch he usually favoured, he insisted on tasting his 'home-made' brew. He made me taste it. Johnny Walker refused, he was not quite so mad. Guru Dutt, on the other hand, was whimsical. His eternal curiosity made him do the strangest things.

~

Abrar also vouches for Johnny Walker's qualities as a human being. In an industry known for its professional jealousies and bickering, Johnny Walker was one person who had no enemies, no one who wanted him to fall. Johnny's biggest rival could have been Mehmood, but Mehmood always called him Johnny Bhai. Mehmood kept in touch with Johnny Walker right to the end and often wrote to Abrar about his Johnny Bhai. In fact, it was Johnny Walker who introduced Mehmood to films via *CID* and Guru Dutt Films. Johnny Walker's humility and simplicity, which came through so eloquently in his performances, is apparent in a couple of anecdotes that Abrar narrates.

One day, Johnny was shooting for a Guru Dutt film and heard a voice calling out 'Badruddin'. He turned to see a burly man gesturing to him. It was the driver of the bus Johnny used to be conductor of. Johnny was genuinely happy to see him and without any starry airs embraced him and made him feel welcome. In fact, it is this 'man-of-the-soil' aspect to his character which came across in his performances and appealed to his fans. I remember when my cousin came to visit Bombay and wanted to see a shoot, he said, 'I want to see Johnny Walker.' I told him I could take him to a set where Dilip Kumar was shooting, and he said, 'That's okay, but I want to see Johnny Walker on a shoot.' Such was the power of this simple man.

14

Kahin Building, Kahin Tramen, Kahin Motor . . .

Kaagaz Ke Phool, launched a year after *Pyaasa*, was Guru Dutt's
most ambitious project. He had been carrying around the story
with him from the time he aspired to be a director, as an assistant
to Gyan Mukherjee. Now, having established himself as a successful
film-maker with a series of box-office hits that had also garnered
critical praise, he wanted to make a film which would overshadow
both *CID* and *Pyaasa*. Guru Dutt Films, he felt, was ready to make
artistic history, break new cinematic ground and usher in a
technical revolution. *Kaagaz Ke Phool*, the slice-of-life story of a
director whose talent goes unrecognized by the financiers who
rule the film industry, would, Guru Dutt decided, be shot in
cinemascope. In Abrar's words, it was a revolutionary concept for
the time.

❦

Cinemascope was not a common medium at that time. Except for
Bombay and perhaps Delhi, there were no cinemascope screens
available, so to be able to show the film all over India it also had to

be shot through a normal lens in the normal screen size. This operation would be both stock- and time-consuming; it would actually mean shooting everything twice.

Once a few scenes of *Kaagaz Ke Phool* were shot, Guru Dutt sought the counsel of M.R. Acharekar with whom he had worked—as also had Raj Kapoor—on some projects. Affectionately called Bhau Sahib, Acharekar, an art director and ex-principal of the J.J. School of Art, was a superlative painter of portraits, and a man whose opinion Guru Dutt trusted.

Guru Dutt met Acharekar at the latter's school, at Shivaji Park, and showed him the rushes in cinemascope. The director must have been dismayed at the response he got from the painter. Acharekar disapproved of the rushes, adding that the framing for cinemascope had to be different than when shooting with a normal lens. Bhau Sahib then went on to demonstrate with drawings how the framing could be effectively done for cinemascope. Guru Dutt took the criticism in his stride. Without a second thought, he scrapped everything he had shot and decided to start afresh.

Not long after, Guru Dutt learnt of a special lens available in Europe. It could convert from normal to cinemascope and vice-versa, and thus would help him save both time and money. He decided to check out this lens and acquire it for his film. He had already booked his ticket to Paris and London when he decided that Abrar Alvi would also accompany him.

It was easier said than done. Abrar had no passport. Getting one was not easy those days. One had to obtain a No Objection Certificate, and the authority who had the power to grant it was the then chief minister of Bombay state, Morarji Desai, not an easy man to influence. Abrar remembers Guru Dutt saying, 'If Abrar can't come, I shall not go too,' and it was at that point that actress Bindu's father-in-law intervened and got Abrar his passport. The duo left for Europe in search of the 'magic' lens. In a way, it was Guru Dutt's escape from the tension that had been slowly and steadily mounting on the home front.

Apart from looking for the lens, Guru Dutt toured London and Paris searching for experiences that he could add to his existing raw material. They went all over Paris, visiting topless shows at Lidos, where the mandatory half pint of champagne was happily downed. Guru Dutt hired an interpreter to go along with them for seven to eight hours a day, and among the things that delighted him were the similarities in the names of things in Hindi and French. Abrar describes it as 'a whirlwind trip, full of new experiences' including an evening with a 'lady of leisure' in Paris.

∼

Guru Dutt laughed a lot over the fact that soap was *savon* in French and *saboon* in Hindi. It showed his childlike delight in small things and his alert sensibilities. He traced the origin of the similarity to the fact that savon was named after the place where it was first manufactured and the word had mutated into saboon. He collected a whole range of such similar sounding words, including *ananas* (pineapple). All this at the cost of a few thousand francs. When something whetted his curiosity, he did not think of the money spent on pursuing it.

One evening Guru Dutt decided to spend some time with a 'lady of leisure', as he called her. He chose his young lady and walked up the rickety wooden steps of the boudoir into her chamber. I stayed behind, as I was not interested in such pursuits, and sat around chatting with the madam who ran the place.

Before long, the young woman and her paramour came down

the steps. The woman seemed really angry. Guru Dutt signalled to me and hastily left the place. I quickly asked the young lady what she was so upset about. 'He wasted my time, all he wanted to do was sit and ask me questions about my life and my profession,' she replied. I realized then that for Guru Dutt this was just another opportunity of satisfying his curiosity and learning first-hand from the experiences and lives of others.

Somewhere along the way I got fed up. I told him, 'You continue searching for your lens, I prefer to see Paris.' I booked a Thomas Cook city tour and took in the sights and sounds like a normal tourist.

The Paris tour over, the duo went to London, where they met someone who would pop in and out of Guru Dutt's life over the coming years. Satish Bhatnagar had moved to London in 1946 to study law, and he was still there when the writer–director duo went across ten years later. In that decade, he had become a Londoner with strong connections in India. Married to Shireen Sayani, cousin of eminent broadcaster Ameen Sayani, Satish was also the secretary of India House.

As a result of the prolonged trip the bonding between Abrar and his producer–director grew more secure, each becoming a perfect foil to the other. The lens, however, remained elusive.

And, finally, *Kaagaz Ke Phool* was shot with two lenses. However, by the time he started shooting the film, Guru Dutt had worked out his shot compositions visually and had mastered the art of shooting in cinemascope. This was vindicated by the Filmfare Award for Best Cinematography that *Kaagaz Ke Phool* won and the fact that even after nearly fifty years the movie remains a veritable lesson in cinematography. Technically, *Kaagaz Ke Phool* remains one of cinema's greats. Guru Dutt pulled out a series of never-before experiments successfully, especially in shot framing, lighting and in song sequences. Abrar throws light on the innovations that marked the picturization of '*Waqt ne kiya*'.

∽

Guru Dutt decided every shot of the films he directed. He would place the camera, work out the shot, choose how close he should go for a close-up; very little was left to the cameraman to decide.

If '*Waqt ne kiya*' is still considered one of the best song picturizations in Indian cinema, there is a reason. Some techniques that Guru Dutt followed in shooting that song had never been used before. Yet today, many of those techniques have almost become passé, thanks to indiscriminate use.

For one, the lighting was dramatic, and in tune with much of the visual effects created by the use of light in the film's many striking moments. It is common knowledge now how the shaft of light that cuts diagonally through the frame was created by placing a mirror at an angle in the skylight that the studio set was fortunate to have, but at that moment, while we were creating the scene, it was cause for much sweat, agony and, finally, excitement. We tried every trick and technique to get the impact Guru Dutt wanted, and eventually it worked. And so wonderfully well.

We first used a 1000 kW light, but it was not enough to create a beam of the intensity the director wanted. Finally we had to think of some other source of light, as artificial light was clearly not going to work. The solution: get the afternoon sun into the studio.

Kaagaz Ke Phool was being shot in Mehboob Studios, where we had earlier shot *Mr and Mrs '55*. Both Guru Dutt and V.K. Murthy knew the studio inside out. It was a modern studio, with a sloping roof, a terrace above it and a skylight. Guru Dutt got a huge mirror and two or three smaller ones made in order to create a never-before lighting effect for his song. He suggested the mirrors be so placed that the largest one, on the terrace, would deflect the sunlight on to the smaller ones which, acting like reflectors, would send the beam of light into the studio through the skylight. It was masterly.

I learnt a lot about lighting from him. It came in handy while directing *Sahib Bibi Aur Ghulam*. But I could never really rise to his standard of using light in a scene to make it unique and painterly.

Even more unusual was the fact that for the first time a song was shot that explored the emotional mood of the protagonists. There had been songs that were played in the background, third-party songs so to speak, where the lyrics either spoke to or about the actor or actress on screen and these were usually filmed in long-shots. Guru Dutt took the idea one step further. He had the two protagonists voicing their emotions as if subconsciously without moving their lips. Expounding the personal feelings of both characters without them actually moving their lips was something absolutely fresh and new at that time.

Not all of Guru Dutt's experiments with light and technology were successful though. Abrar mentions how Guru Dutt felt constantly driven to reproduce the feel and finish of Hollywood films. Together with his cameraman Murthy he would sit for hours working out the lighting and thinking up new techniques. He was fascinated by the matte technique that he had experimented with in *Baaz* to create a sense of ships being tossed around in a stormy sea. The result was far from satisfactory, and only a fleeting segment was kept to inform the viewer of the progression of the tale. Now, with *Kaagaz Ke Phool* ready to roll, Murthy was sent abroad to work and learn more about the matte technique from J. Lee Thomson, who later directed *The Guns of Navarone*.

One of the experiments in matte technique that Guru Dutt tried in *Kaagaz Ke Phool* was with the comedian Vasari, who was known as the king of comedy before Johnny Walker became a household name. Guru Dutt visualized a scene where the hero would grapple with his conscience. The matte technique could create a double image, one normal and the other small, and show the two interacting with each other.

Guru Dutt wanted Vasari the 'conscience' to jump on to the hero's knee, then to his lap, then on to his shoulder to whisper in his ear. The cinematographer and the director worked on the scene for fifteen days, but in the end the experiment had to be scrapped. Whatever they did, they could not remove the white line of the matting that divided the figures and showed the patchwork. Unhappy with the result and unwilling to compromise on quality, the director decided to dump the scene.

Much later, Guru Dutt would abandon another ambitious project, called *Gangasagar*, only because he was aware of the inadequacies of filming sea scenes, and the climax of that film revolved around a shipwreck.

15

Chaudhvin Ka Chand Ho . . .

One of Guru Dutt's most popular films at the time of its release was *Chaudhvin Ka Chand*. Written by Shaukat Hussain Rizvi, husband of the singer Noorjehan, the story and script of the film were owned by Asia Theatres, as the writer had migrated to Pakistan. Rizvi had a fairly good reputation as a writer. *Khandan* (1942), written and directed by him with Pran and Noorjehan in the lead, had been a thundering success.

Guru Dutt bought the script from Asia Theatres for the princely sum of five thousand rupees. Only to discover that it was written in Urdu. He did not have the patience to go through the tome. That was when Abrar came into the picture. Being on the payrolls of Guru Dutt Films, he was given the task of translating the Urdu script, complete with dialogues, into English. True to character, Abrar translated the entire work, and added a few touches of his own, 'especially to add force to the dialogues', as he says.

Ek Jhalak, as the script was then titled, was the story of two friends—one rich, and the other, the hero, poor enough to be deeply indebted, emotionally, to his friend. At the *navchandi mela*, the rich friend happens to spot the hero's wife and falls in love with her. She knows who he is, having seen him from behind the curtains, visiting her husband in their house. But, of course, he does not know her real identity or her relationship with his friend.

She tells her husband about his friend seeing her face. When in turn the rich friend raves about the woman he has had a glimpse of (the 'Ek Jhalak' of the title), and has fallen in love with, the hero is unable to tell him that the woman is his wife. Instead, he tells his wife he will divorce her, so she can marry his friend. Needless to say, the wife complicates matters by refusing to accept the idea.

The hero writes a letter, willing his wife to marry his friend, then tells the friend that the woman he desires has agreed to marry him and that he should take a baraat and go to her place. When the baraat comes, the hero removes himself from the scene by committing suicide. The wife, newly widowed and, thanks to her husband's will, about to be married again, cannot take the double shock, and dies of a heart attack. The story ends with the hero's friend in the graveyard, praying for the dead couple at their graves.

Abrar recounts the events that led to the restructuring of *Ek Jhalak* into *Chaudhvin Ka Chand*.

❧

I could not stand the mood of the story. I asked Guru Dutt about the logic behind two people dying, and a third man being left with nothing. It had nothing to offer the viewer, expect a pointlessly sad story.

For six years I would not let the film, now titled *Chaudhvin Ka Chand*, be made. I said, 'Muslims do not really believe that their women are like a pair of shoes.' I felt it was completely wrong to let a man, the hero of a film, pass on his wife to another man. I said, 'This writer has run off to Pakistan and left this third-rate story behind.' I also pointed out the anomalies to Guru Dutt. Here is a man pining for a woman after a single jhalak . . . and look at him, hale and hearty, eating and drinking, and even singing songs.

I had a problem even with the film's title. There is no connection between the title and the story of the film. In fact, *Chaudhvin Ka Chand* was the title I had given to a story of mine based on a Japanese story called 'The Jade Goddess'; I had turned the theme around and Indianized it, replacing the jade carver in the original with a poet and singer. All at Guru Dutt's request. The climax of that story happened on the night of the 'chaudhvin ka chand', and hence the title. But Guru Dutt scrapped the idea of filming that story, though he registered the title, *Chaudhvin Ka Chand*, as his property.

I was friendly with Saghir Usmani who had been called to work on the film, but I told him that I could not be false to my profession. I did not believe in this love at first jhalak. Such intensity of emotion is not logical. Even Laila and Majnu had a love that grew out of their childhood . . . this story defied logic. You are putting an elephant on a tendril, I added, and building a climax on a whim . . . it will not wash with audiences. I washed my hands off the film. I refused to have anything to do with the ridiculous story.

But Guru Dutt, even as he heard Abrar out, wanted to get on with the film. *Kaagaz Ke Phool* had flopped; he needed a hit badly, and he needed to work to keep his unit solvent. He was also sure he wanted his best writer involved in its production. When he insisted, Abrar put forth his theory once more, more forcefully. 'I told them, this movie won't work with the hero and heroine dead. If you have to kill someone, kill the man, let him die of shame for coveting a friend's wife. Though, I added, I am not even convinced of his sense of shame.'

Luckily for the fate of the film, Guru Dutt paid heed this time, and the script was turned around. Johnny Walker had a brilliant role carved out for him. Guru Dutt played the hero, and Waheeda his lovely but confused wife. Rehman was cast as the rich friend, and looked the part every inch. Abrar wrote the screenplay, the dialogues were rewritten by Tabish Sultanpuri, and the film went on the floors. Though the film's direction is officially credited to M. Sadiq, it bears Guru Dutt's stamp all over. *Chaudhvin Ka Chand* showcased Guru Dutt's exquisite handling of song sequences. It has cinematography that once again proved that Guru Dutt was a master of lighting as well as of shot composition. And there is evidence of his growing fascination for his new heroine in the way the camera moves over her face ever so lovingly in the title song sequence and lingers on her features to catch every passing mood they reflect.

Guru Dutt was also aware of the importance of the Muslim audience and their tendency to see the films that caught their fancy more than once. He displayed exceeding care and sensitivity for the Muslim way of life and portrayed it with great empathy. 'It was,' Abrar says, 'the first really good and true-to-life Muslim social to hit the screen in fifteen years, and it was a hit beyond our expectations.'

Abrar was not involved with *Chaudhvin Ka Chand* on the sets. In fact, after the reshaping of the screenplay, he hurried off to write the scripts of *Suraj* and *Saathi* for Venus Films. But he has an interesting story to tell about the making of the title song, which proved to be the film's biggest highlight.

❧

Ravi, the music director, had been given the task of creating the musical score for the film. He composed the tune of the title song and played it for Guru Dutt. To his dismay, Guru Dutt rejected it and told him to go back and work on some other ideas for the song.

Ravi had created a few alternatives, but was sure his original tune was a winner. He came to me saying, 'You have great influence with Guru Dutt. Will you sit in on this session and give him your views?'

The session started. Ravi played the new tune. Guru Dutt listened intently. There was no knowing what his reaction was, he could be poker faced when the whim took him. Ravi looked at me, helplessness eloquent in his eyes. It was time for me to do something. I asked him to play some other alternatives. 'Is there nothing else?' I asked, seemingly innocently. Ravi, quick to take the cue, played his original tune.

I listened and said, 'Aha, this is so much better, I am sure this will work.' Guru Dutt looked at me and said, 'Okay, let us go with this for now, let us picturize it and see how it shapes up.' I think Ravi could have danced with joy at that point.

Ravi's faith in his music was vindicated when the song '*Chaudhvin ka chand ho ya aftaab ho*' became an all-time hit. Among the best love songs that Mohammad Rafi has sung, it won two Filmfare Awards: Rafi for best singer and Shakeel Badayuni for best lyricist. Ravi, unfortunately, did not get an award for his composition. The film also won art director Biren Nag a Filmfare Award.

16

Jadoo Nagri Se Aaya Hai
Koi Jadoogar

In his ability to use music to take a tale forward, Guru Dutt perhaps has few parallels. To him the song was essential to the film's theme, and its picturization a challenge that brought out the best in him as a film-maker. The song in a Guru Dutt film was not a filler or an 'interval' for the audience to step out for a quick smoke. It helped in characterization, in adding suspense, in making the plot move to the next level and, of course, sometimes in introducing a character to the audience.

Whoever the music director he worked with—S.D. Burman, O.P. Nayyar, Ravi—Guru Dutt had the ability to make their songs come alive on screen in a way then unique to cinema. And whoever his music director, Guru Dutt had his say, often making them bend to his will. Thus it was that O.P. Nayyar adapted a tune Guru Dutt had taken a fancy to, 'Clementine', to create the now-immortal 'Zara hat ke, zara bach ke, yeh hai Bombay meri jaan' (CID) and S.D. Burman had to work around a tune from Harry Black and the Tiger, which was recreated as 'Sar jo tera chakraye' (Pyaasa). Interestingly enough, both songs were filmed on Johnny Walker.

If Guru Dutt used the music of O.P. Nayyar in his more playful

comedies like *Mr and Mrs '55* and the breezy *CID*, he signed on
S.D. Burman for *Pyaasa*. Guru Dutt had worked with SD in both
Baazi and *Jaal*, which he had directed for friend Dev Anand, and
he must have believed that the soulfulness of the Bengali musician
would fit in well with the mood of this story. Besides, Guru Dutt
wanted to use a chakla of Sahir's which had been composed much
before *Pyaasa* was conceived, and which proved to be a turning
point in the making of the film and its tone. The Sahir–S.D. Burman
team had worked well in *Baazi* and *Jaal*. Thus, the choice of one
made the other inevitable.

Though Abrar's professional interaction with S.D. Burman and
Sahir began in right earnest only with *Pyaasa*, Abrar had first met
Sahir in 1951, at a meeting of the Poets and Writers' Association.

He had a big nose which caught my attention. We were to become
good friends. Sahir drove a Fiat those days, and smoked a lot,
though he was trying to kick the habit. He would break a cigarette
neatly in half, so neatly that it looked as if it had been cut with a
knife. And despite his serious bent of mind when it came to poetry,
Sahir loved to pull a susceptible person's leg, and would do so with
a disarming smile that threw the person completely off guard.

Sahir had rather strong views about the importance of the
lyricist vis-à-vis the music director, views that rubbed many people
the wrong way. He would hotly defend the lyricist's position as
superior to the music director's. Songwriters have to use their
intellect, while music directors only play one instrument, the
gramophone, he'd aver, sarcastically referring to the fact that music
directors often listened to English records for 'inspiration'. And thus
he would insist stubbornly on being paid a rupee more than what
the music director was paid for a movie.

Such conditions and convictions got him on the wrong side of many music directors of his time. One day, while we were all together, he got a bit high and aired his views on music directors being lesser mortals to writers like him. S.D. Burman, who was present, got very riled up about his statements. Dada pronounced then and there that he would never again work with Sahir, not for the rest of his life.

～

It was a crisis indeed. *Pyaasa* was under way, and the last song was yet to be written. Guru Dutt and Abrar worked hard at mollifying S.D. Burman, and he softened to a degree. But he agreed only to set music to Sahir's words. He would not sit with him to create the number. That was when Sahir wrote his immortal lyrics of the embittered poet of *Pyaasa* returning to grace his own death anniversary function. And that was when Abrar's absence due to hospitalization led to Sahir's lyrics creating an anachronism in time and place. Though the SD–Sahir partnership came undone after *Pyaasa*, thanks to Sahir's views, Abrar has fond memories of the poet.

～

Sahir was a straightforward person; he was incapable of flattery, but he managed to surround himself with flatterers. But they did serve an end. When there was no one else around to satisfy his yen for practical jokes, he would pull their leg instead. The poet never married, but his lady fans were legion. And the reason for his single status also ran true to his nature.

Sahir had a weak heart. Doctors had told him that he could have a heart attack any time; so he did not want to leave a widow behind. But he had a strong and abiding relationship with the poet Amrita Pritam, which enriched the life and work of both.

〜

Abrar was twenty-six years old when he worked with S.D. Burman for the first time, during the making of *Pyaasa*. Something in their chemistry worked wonderfully, to the extent that Abrar could take the liberty of teasing the music director and even play pranks on him. The rapport between the fifty-year-old maestro and the young writer comes through in the many anecdotes Abrar recounts, stories that reveal the inherent simplicity of S.D. Burman as a man, a simplicity that is reflected in his music too.

〜

I had heard a lot about S.D. Burman, the composer. Guru Dutt was very fond of him and admired his work immensely, but could not refrain from adding that the man was very *kanjoos*. He once narrated an episode from their early days of collaboration. Guru Dutt was working on *Baazi* at that time and, along with his assistants, used to visit Dada at his place to discuss the musical score and other relevant details about the film. Dada had a room at Khar Hotel, a longish building along the road, with rooms on top and an eating house on the ground floor where boarders could have their meals.

One day, the sitting went on for a long time, and Guru Dutt started feeling hungry. Dada had obviously had his lunch early, as was his habit. Finally, unable to bear the hunger pangs, Guru Dutt told his host, 'Please order something; get us some food from the place below, we are all hungry.'

Dada went to the balcony and looked down, then turned back to look at his director and said, 'Hungry, hmmm . . .' He called the errand boy, gave him four annas and said, 'There's a *bhuttawala* down there, get some *bhuttas*.' He then turned to ask Guru Dutt whether he liked the corn ripe or tender. 'Do you like yellow *danas* or white?' he asked his director, who could only stare astounded.

Later, during the recording for *Pyaasa*, Dada used to take a train every day, and it bothered him that he had to shell out the money for a rickshaw from the station and back, day after day. He hated parting with his money. Sunit Kar, his assistant, would cycle to the studio as he lived closer. One day, Dada saw the bike and told Sunit, 'Your bike has a carrier, I will hitch a ride every day with you to and from the station.' And that was that. He never took a cycle rickshaw after that, unless for some reason Sunit was not available.

Then there were the times Guru Dutt and I would visit Dada at his house. Dada had made his name in the world of Hindi film music by then. He had moved out of his hotel room at Khar and had his own house, where he lived with his family. The room we sat in was partitioned by a curtain from the dining area. We'd be there at lunchtime and there would be a call for lunch from the other side of the partition. Dada would get up and go to the other side, from where he'd ask in Bengali, 'Will you eat something?' Guru Dutt would quickly respond, 'No, you eat.' I loved to tease him, but he was always game. I would call out to him, 'Don't ask me, I am hungry and I will say yes and come across to join you.' He'd say, 'No, I'm not asking you.'

Dada never really got upset with my pranks. He was very fond of me, very protective, like an elder brother. Dada loved paan; he would carry it with him everywhere. He'd place the packets containing his paan on one side while he played on his harmonium, and look at them time and again to make sure they had not gone missing.

Even when Dada came to Guru Dutt's office, he would carry three to four packets of paan, wrapped in dry leaves, and his scented tobacco would be in a separate packet. No one would touch his paans. Sometimes when he got busy with his music, and was too engrossed to notice anything else, I would slip towards the paan packets lying by his side, open a packet and call out to him, 'Dada, *paan chori ho rahi hai* (someone is stealing your paan).' Dada would jump up with a start. '*Kaun chori karta* (who is stealing),' he'd ask, and I'd answer, 'It's me, *main paan chura raha hoon . . .*' He'd frown, then say, '*Chura, par aur kuch mat churao* (steal it then, but don't steal anything else).' And I would eat a paan.

The only thing that could upset him was an adverse comment about his music, even if made in jest. But even then, he would be almost childlike in his reactions. I remember, during the shooting of *Pyaasa* at Kardar Studio, they were rehearsing '*Jaane kya tune kahi*', which Geeta Dutt was to sing. Sahir and I were sitting in the veranda at the back, away from the rehearsal.

We could hear the music filtering through from inside, 'dhun dhun dhun'. At first it was only the orchestra, then the orchestra with the vocals. I commented off-hand to Sahir, 'What sort of music is Dada making—it makes me think of horses in a circus ring.' At that moment, Dada came out to spit his tobacco. He lifted his hand towards us to signal, 'Wait, I'm coming.' I told Sahir to keep quiet about my comment, but Sahir was not to be silenced.

When Dada came towards us saying, 'What are you talking about?' Sahir piped up, 'He says you are making circus music.'

Dada's fair skin turned red, he moved menacingly towards me, finger raised threateningly. I expected to be slapped, but he came close to my face and said, '*Tum, tum . . . tum jab picture direct karega, main uska music nahin doonga.*' He wouldn't score the music when I directed a film. It was his extreme threat, the worst he could think of!

S.D. Burman was a simple and innocent soul. Guru Dutt used to get a thrill out of pulling his leg, and of course I would pitch in. It was always done with due respect—innocent fun at Dada's expense.

Once we were all sitting at a music session; Pancham, Dada's son, was at the tabla, Sunit, Guru Dutt and I were all sitting around with Dada. We kept asking him, how do we fit the dance action to the song—we kept teasing him, asking him, 'How will she dance in joy to the music, we cannot visualize it . . .' Dada actually got up in his dhoti and kurta and started dancing. Mind you, his movements were quite kuccha, but he had a terrific sense of rhythm. We had to try hard to control our laughter . . .

Also, when he was composing or singing, he had the knack of getting totally lost in his taans. When he sang, it was worth not just listening to him but seeing him at it—his right hand would be at his ear, his left hand stretched out, and then he would move both hands rhythmically.

In 1962, Dada announced that he was planning a tour of Europe with his wife. Everything connected with his travel was fixed to the last detail with his travel agent. 'Get all the work you need done, I won't be around for two months,' he announced. Guru Dutt decided to have some fun.

I started by saying, 'The Chinese war is on, people are condemning the Chinese. Please don't mind, I'm saying this because I am concerned, you look more Chinese than Indian and people might end up treating you badly because they hate what the Chinese are doing to an innocent country, and Bhabhi won't be able to help you much either.'

The joke backfired. Dada began to seriously reconsider the trip. Guru Dutt asked me, 'What have you done?' We had to set about reassuring him and telling him that we had only been pulling his leg. He was so gullible and trusting and childlike, such endearing traits. He was a lovable person, totally devoid of all pretences.

Another time, he offered me a lift in his car, a Baby Austin. I told him I was not alone, I had a friend with me. 'Bring him along too,' Dada said magnanimously, 'we will just be four people along with the driver, and that's fine.' But when my friend came up to get into the car, Dada stared at him. I motioned my friend to get into the car but Dada looked at me and told me he wanted to speak to me in private. He took me a little distance away and said, 'It won't do, your friend is too fat, he will ruin my car's springs, they will break!'

Behind all this light-hearted ribbing and playfulness lay the awareness that they were all creating something great, something that would outlive them all. Each of them was dead serious when it came to work, each pulling his weight towards the realization of the classics they created. Abrar, though a writer, would be involved in the music sessions and his interventions often came in handy, as they did in the creation of one of Hindi cinema's greatest songs.

During the making of *Kaagaz Ke Phool*, Kaifi Azmi was stuck at a point for the right words for a song. Dada kept humming the tune he had composed, 'tarra rum, tarra rum . . .' but no one could get the hang of the actual tune. So Dada went a step ahead, he put Bengali and Hindi words to the tune: 'Khao re, khao re, bhajiya . . .'

Kaifi was not so used to the music part of composing a song. He was not as sharp or quick as Sahir was, though his poetry is beautiful and very special. I removed the 'bhajiyas' Dada had put in and wrote false words for the song, so that Kaifi could fill in the blanks. The words I composed went thus: '*Aaj hum gaya, waqt tham gaya, aap aaye gaye, dard tham gaya.*' The words were near nonsense, but they filled out Dada's tune. And Kaifi got his impetus from them.

The song was finally composed: '*Waqt ne kiya, kya haseen situm, tum rahen na tum, hum rahen na hum*', a song that still moves hearts with its lyrics and tune. But there was a problem at the time. Kaifi's lyrics cut Dada's tune short, the 'tum' at the end left the tune short of one syllable. Dada had tuned Abrar's words, pulling out the 'gaya' beautifully. Now he had to shorten the line, sacrifice the length of his note, but being the genius he was, he made it work.

According to Abrar, S.D. Burman was not just *sureela* as a singer and musician, he was *raseela* too. There was soul in his compositions and in his rendering of them. 'When he sang to explain a tune to the playback singer, he would often overshadow the singer,' Abrar remembers. 'Sometimes one felt that he ought to sing most of his songs himself.'

When *Baharen Phir Bhi Aayengi* was being planned, Guru Dutt started, as was his habit, with the songs, and set about recording them. S.D. Burman was his obvious choice for music director, but unfortunately, Dada fell ill after composing one number for the film. As usual, Guru Dutt could not wait. If he hit upon something he had to do it as soon as possible. He handed the music over to O.P. Nayyar, with whom he had worked in *Aar Paar* and *Mr and Mrs '55*. The song that S.D. Burman had composed for *Baharen*, which remained unused in the film, was later shot on Dev Anand in *Jewel Thief*. The song: 'Yeh dil na hota bechaara.'

There were other songs by SD that Guru Dutt rejected. '*Rangeela re*', which became a hit in the film *Prem Pujari*, was one such. 'I liked the song a lot and tried to get Guru Dutt to keep it,' Abrar says, 'but he would have none of it. We went to Lonavala, and I kept humming the song, and Guru Dutt said, "Whose song is it, not Dada's?" I told him, "It's the song you rejected." He agreed then that it was a nice song. Dada's music grew on you.'

17

Waqt Ne Kiya
Kya Haseen Situm

Despite his dreams for the film, *Kaagaz Ke Phool* ended up a disaster. There was no hint in the popular and critical response to the film at the time that it would become one of India's best-known films and be seen as a landmark in film-making. In fact, Guru Dutt had to face the ignominy of audiences throwing shoes at the screen or booing the hero as he appeared on screen.

While Guru Dutt has gone on record admitting that the movie 'went over the heads' of his audience, Abrar believes that one of the reasons for the failure of *Kaagaz Ke Phool* was that the audience could not identify with the mental angst of a man who was a 'khaata pita admi', well-off, well-to-do, but unhappy over his lack of intellectual and creative freedom. In a country where the masses were still concerned about getting their daily meal and struggling with abject poverty, this unhappiness seemed abstract and self-indulgent. Critics panned the film as narcissist and self-pitying, and Guru Dutt was naturally devastated. He was also close to being financially crippled, and the fact that he had to keep his studio running and find the wherewithal to pay his team of loyal workers, added to his despair and despondency.

❦

When *Kaagaz Ke Phool* bombed, Guru Dutt Films was naturally strapped for money. It was around this time that after two months of not being able to pay salaries, Guru Dutt sent me a letter that read, 'You know the company is passing through a lean phase. You, at a salary of 2500, are among the highest paid; if you can supplement your income, it will be a great help.'

The message was clear. I was being given permission to work outside the banner. I took up an assignment with Madhubala, as the implication of Guru Dutt's letter was that no salary should be expected from Guru Dutt Films as there was no film on the floors. *Chaudhvin Ka Chand* was being made; my role in it was not official. I was not the writer of the film, and was seen on the sets only as a well-wisher. Of course, I did have a role to play in turning the original story around, but that was in an unofficial capacity, because I was part of Guru Dutt Films.

It was not tough for me to get assignments with other banners. As far as the industry was concerned, I had arrived. So I graduated from a salaried man on the rolls of Guru Dutt Films to a contract writer, free to choose his subject and director.

❦

Thus it came to be that Abrar Alvi was not an employee of Guru Dutt Films at the initial planning stage of *Sahib Bibi Aur Ghulam*. Yet, to his surprise Abrar got a call from Guru Dutt asking him to write the screenplay for *Sahib Bibi Aur Ghulam*, Guru Dutt Films' next project. Guru Dutt had read the novel and seen the play in Calcutta in the original Bengali. It had never been translated into Hindi or any other language. He wanted Abrar to work on the script. The writer was flummoxed.

❦

'How do I read the novel?' I asked. 'It is in Bengali!' Guru Dutt decided to work on the story with me. He tried to translate the novel by reading and paraphrasing it for me, but the process was painstaking and very slow. We tried it for a few days and realized it would not work.

He then summoned Bimal Mitra, the writer of the novel, and got him down from Calcutta. A bungalow was rented in Khandala for a year. Guru Dutt always looked into every aspect of a project, and did not stint on details or expenses; the bungalow would ensure that Bimal Mitra and I worked in complete seclusion till we had the script ready.

We repaired to Khandala—Bimal Mitra, myself and the novel. Along with us came one Mr Mukherjee, whose reason for being around was that he was conversant in both Bengali and Hindi. Bimal Babu was not very fluent in either Hindi or English, and Mr Mukherjee was expected to be the bridge between us.

But after fifteen days or so, Mr Mukherjee decided he had had enough, and I offered to cope with the translation and Bimal Babu all by myself. Slowly but surely, the screenplay took shape. I took a few artistic licences in the interest of Hindi cinema, keeping its audience in mind. I cut out a few characters, like that of Swami Vivekananda, who featured in the novel through almost a hundred pages.

The story is set in the Calcutta of the late 1800s, but there was little cohesion in the original story and it would not have worked as a Hindi film. I had to add some aspects to the storyline to make it hold together, and Bimal Babu went along with the changes quite willingly.

For example, in the original novel, the hero is not quite the country yokel he is in the film. But I painted his character the way it was filmed, with his noisy shoes and his somewhat vacant look at the beginning of the film, to introduce a bit of lightness. Also in the film's final shape, I did away with the role of a comedian. I preferred to put in the humour into characters and their interactions. Of course, it was a tough decision, especially knowing Guru Dutt's fondness for Johnny Walker and his superstition about having a role for him in every film made under his banner.

Guru Dutt kept saying, '*Johnny ka role likho, Johnny ke liye role nikalo,*' but I resisted. I told him I will explain to Johnny, and he will understand that there is no scope for him in this film.

❧

So the two writers sat together and found a central theme, isolated it from the novel and then hammered out a screenplay. And as he wrote it, Abrar ensured that he imbued the character of the protagonist, which was played later by Guru Dutt himself, with a lightness that would be a perfect foil for the grand tragedy of Chhoti Bahu.

For the first time in the history of Guru Dutt Films, a script was ready ahead of shooting. *Sahib Bibi Aur Ghulam* was written to the last detail, ready to go on the floors. Guru Dutt then proceeded to ensure he had the same people behind the scenes—the cinematographer, the art director, the editor—who had lent his earlier films an artistic cohesiveness, the look which said 'A Guru Dutt film'.

❧

I was allowed to go back to my freelance work outside Guru Dutt Films, but, to ensure he had my expertise in handling dialogues, Guru Dutt asked me to record the entire script on spool. He came to me and said, 'I have got used to your presence on the sets. I want you to record the entire script, as you have written and conceived the film. If needed, rerecord it as many times as you wish, till you are satisfied.' His exact words were, '*Jaise ke tum ne likha hai, usi effect tape pe lao.*'

It took all of three weeks to get the entire film on to a spool. We recorded it in the studio most professionally, and once it was done, Guru Dutt would listen to it many times over. I used all my histrionic talents, and all the experience I had with radio and theatre through my college years. I recorded the film completely, speaking all the dialogues in different voices. I could see Guru Dutt was impressed. He would hide his eyes in the crook of his arm, a very typical stance, and listen to how the dialogues were delivered.

∾

Sahib Bibi Aur Ghulam brought to a head Guru Dutt's obsession with Bengal. Despite his Bengali-sounding name, Guru Dutt was not a Bengali. A Saraswat Brahmin from Mangalore, his mother tongue was Konkani, and his family name Padukone bore evidence of the village his ancestors hailed from.

Guru Dutt had spent many of his formative years in Calcutta though, and could thus read and write the Bengali script. His mother, a teacher in Calcutta, was also a linguist; she could fluently converse in and read five languages—Hindi, English, Kannada, Marathi and Bengali—a gift that Guru Dutt admired immensely.

It is not clear at which point in his life Guru Dutt dropped the Padukone from his name and broke the single word 'Gurudutt' into two words, to give his name a Bengali flavour, but it reflected his fascination for Bengal and all the things that were linked to its art and culture and language. A fascination that is evident in almost all his films and one which Abrar vouches for.

∾

Pyaasa, for instance, had no links with Bengal. The poetry was in Hindi with marked Urdu overtones, the 'chakla' that Sahir had in his private collection and which Guru Dutt wanted to use as a powerful statement in his film was in Hindustani, and referred to the typically central Indian way of life, yet when the film was shot, Guru Dutt chose to go across to Calcutta for location shooting. The entire unit was taken to Calcutta and scenes were written so that the city's many backdrops could form the canvas for the film.

Take the shot where Guru Dutt meets his brothers at the Ganga ghat after they have immersed their mother's ashes. It was written just so he could shoot in the Calcutta ghats. Sometimes, of course, his obsession with Bengal could result in strange mistakes.

I was overseeing *Pyaasa* all through, but at one point I had to go away for a few weeks for my operation. Guru Dutt had signed on Mehmood to play the second brother of the protagonist. It was Mehmood's first shoot, and he wanted to show how thorough an actor he was and plunge into the character given to him. He reportedly asked where the shot was situated, and when he learnt it was in Calcutta, he decided to flaunt a Bengali accent.

I was the person responsible for the details of accents and diction; my absence resulted in Mehmood talking like a Bengali while the rest of the family, including his mother and brothers, were very obviously from Benares. By the time I could point out the anomaly, the shot had been canned, and it was too late. The discrepancy remains to this day!

18

Bhanwara Bada Nadaan Hai

Guru Dutt now started casting for his new film. Having seen Bengali actor Biswajeet in the play version, he thought seriously about casting him as Bhootnath, the country bumpkin who comes to the city, looking for work. He also wanted to sign Chhaya Arya, wife of photographer Jitendra Arya, for the part of Chhoti Bahu.

Chhaya Arya was living with her husband in London at the time. It was an ambitious project and a challenging role, and when the Aryas were asked to relocate from UK and settle in Bombay so that Chhaya could work in the film, they hesitated but came along nonetheless. Abrar recalls the Aryas arriving in Khandala where Guru Dutt made them listen to the spools Abrar had recorded. 'I remember how Jitendra, after listening to the tape, asked me who had spoken for Chhoti Bahu. He was quite amazed when I told him that all the voices in the spool were mine.' Guru Dutt also wanted Abrar to play the role of Ghadi Babu, a part that later went to Harindranath Chattopadhyay.

By the time the film went on the floors, much of the casting was to change dramatically.

Though it was natural for Guru Dutt to take on the direction and he had been working towards that end, Abrar says that he was not in a frame of mind conducive to wielding the directorial baton.

He decided to approach Satyen Bose to direct the film. Bose agreed but insisted he would get his unit along. But Guru Dutt would have none of that—he had his own loyal unit and was in turn loyal to them. He next approached Nitin Bose, who listened in all earnestness to the tape and then went silent without giving a response for three months. Guru Dutt got the message, though unspoken, that Nitin Bose was not interested in the project. That was when he decided that his new film would be directed by Abrar Alvi.

∽

Guru Dutt dropped in one evening. He frequently dropped by at my place when he wanted peace and quiet from the stream of visitors who thronged his house, so I was not surprised. We would sit quietly and share a drink, and talk a little of this and that. But that evening he seemed to have something on his mind.

'What have you got to offer me?' he asked.

'I don't have Scotch, I can offer Indian,' I replied.

We sat down over a drink, when he suddenly said, 'It's not working. Why don't you do it, direct the film?'

I said, 'Why, what's the problem? Why don't you do it? I have already done the recording for you.'

He replied, 'I don't want to—I don't feel like it. Why don't you do it?' he asked me again. '*Jaisa tum ne likha hai, jaisa tum ne bola hai*, just bring that on screen and I will be satisfied.'

I laughed. 'You are being emotional, this is not going to work. The drink you have had is talking, not you.'

He was very sensitive. My reproach hurt him. He sat silent for a while, then got up and left.

He came back after three or four days and we had something of a repeat performance. He insisted I direct; I remonstrated. He said again, 'I know you can do it.' Again, when I turned him down, he retreated into his cocoon, and then left.

The next day, his driver, Ramji, came over. 'Sahab wants you to go to his office before lunch, he has sent me to fetch you,' he said.

So I got into the car and reached his office at about eleven-thirty. He was sitting behind his table on his usual chair under the blow-up of his guru, Gyan Mukherjee. He was dripping sarcasm undiluted. 'Arrey, come, come,' he said, 'let's get the red carpet out for our guest.' I was nonplussed, but sat down opposite him.

He beckoned me closer. 'Come here,' he said, 'smell my mouth, my breath. Do you smell liquor?' I shook my head. 'Leave aside your nakhras,' he continued. 'I am speaking here in front of a witness. I want you to direct my film. Will you?'

'If you think I can, I will,' I responded.

His friend, Ram Singh, an actor he had befriended during his Prabhat days, butted in. 'Why don't you direct it yourself?' he asked Guru Dutt. 'Have you forgotten direction?'

Guru Dutt replied that he did not wish to take on the responsibility.

Ram Singh continued, 'It's a difficult subject and Abrar won't be able to handle it either. Give him a comedy or something light, not something as heavy and complicated. After all, this is his first directorial venture . . .'

Guru Dutt cut him short. 'Don't challenge me, Ram Singh,' he said. 'I can take any bet on Abrar delivering the goods.'

I think at that moment Guru Dutt had more confidence in me than I had in myself.

Once the film was handed over to Abrar, things started moving. The first set for shooting was situated in Bombay, where all of Waheeda's scenes would be shot. And it is in Waheeda's casting that one discerns one of the many frictions that were part of the shoot. Abrar is emphatic that she wasn't entirely suited to the role. He feels that given due scope, and if Guru Dutt had not come in the way, he could have got a more credible performance out of the actress.

There were other changes on the cards.

The stills of Chhaya Arya displeased Guru Dutt. He found her 'jawline too pronounced, her face too harsh on camera'. She was glamorous and beautiful in real life, but Guru Dutt wanted Chhoti Bahu to look wanton and motherly and beseeching all rolled in one at different times, and Chhaya's face seemed incapable of at least some of the softness and yearning that the character demanded. Abrar narrates some of the casting woes that marked the making of *Sahib Bibi Aur Ghulam*.

Waheeda is a fine artist and I could get almost anything out of her. But I still believe she was miscast as Jaba. Her personality was not suited for the role of a mischievous girl with a mercurial temperament. A Madhubala or a Geeta Bali could have done the role so much better.

Meanwhile, the relationship between the two had blossomed and Guru Dutt was very possessive of her and kept directing her through the scenes. Needless to say, he was also seeing her role through his eyes and not the way I wanted her character to be played. That is why I feel she did not rise to her role as well as she had done in her earlier films.

Coming to Chhaya, I told Guru Dutt that I would get her to emote, that he should not drop her. 'I will be blamed for dropping her after she has uprooted herself from her home in London,' I said, but he was ruthless. I have never known a more uncompromising director. He spared no one, not his own wife, whom he cast in a film called *Gauri* only to scrap it when it did not measure up to his expectations; not even himself, when he found his acting inadequate in *Raaz*, of which he had shot twelve reels!

❦

Dropping Chhaya Arya as Chhoti Bahu and signing Waheeda Rehman as Jaba meant that Abrar began the film with two handicaps: the absence of a heroine for the film's central character and a less-than-perfect choice for the other major female role. Then there was also the matter of looking for someone to play the hero.

Rehman and Sapru had been decided upon for the other major male characters, but the role of Bhootnath was still to find an anchor. Abrar approached Shashi Kapoor at Mohan Studios where he was shooting and fixed an appointment with him, asking him to come across and listen to the tape. Shashi Kapoor seemed impressed enough with the role and went back to consider taking on the project.

But Guru Dutt had other plans. Geeta had been telling him to take on the hero's mantle. He had, after all, successfully played the lead in *Pyaasa*, *Kaagaz Ke Phool* and *Chaudhvin Ka Chand*, and she fancied being the wife of an actor rather than a director. Moreover, it would save money and the interminable wait for dates. Besides, Guru Dutt was the producer of the film and when the producer wants to play the lead, the director has to bow to his wishes. Abrar was no exception though he had a precondition which he put down with characteristic directness.

❦

I thought seriously about casting Shashi Kapoor. The actor turned up a few hours late, and I remember taunting him, asking how he would be able to come on time through the weeks of shooting if on the first day he was three hours late. We put the tape on at seven-fifteen p.m. and wound down three hours later. Shashi Kapoor promised to get back with his decision but in the meantime Guru Dutt decided to take on the role himself.

I personally wasn't keen on Guru Dutt playing Bhootnath, or, for that matter, the hero in even my comedies. I felt and still feel that as an actor he was stilted, and his real talent lay in direction. However, I agreed on one condition. I told him, 'The hero is a country yokel, he is callow and unsure of himself. You have to look the part. Your moustache makes your face heavy. You need to shave it off.'

Thus, to play Bhootnath, Guru Dutt removed the moustache that had characterized his persona as the hero in all his earlier films. 'The moustache never came back,' Abrar says with a chuckle. Shooting started in earnest, in Bombay, on the first of January 1961, a date chosen by Guru Dutt because it symbolized a beginning: the start of a new year. But if the casting issues were sorted, other prickly matters remained which cast their shadows on the shoot.

As a director, Guru Dutt took a keen interest in shot-taking. He had the final say on decisions pertaining to camera placements, shots, close-ups. The cameraman would merely follow his instructions. So, when Abrar took on the director's role and started visualizing the shots, some clash of wills seemed inevitable.

I have no doubt that Guru Dutt respected me being the director, but at times there were very obvious and vocal differences between our viewpoints. This one scene in particular, when Jaba's father dies, where in the outer room, Jaba's fiancé Supavitra is asleep and Bhootnath is restlessly pacing. In the inner room, Jaba's father is lying in bed, obviously very sick. Jaba is nearby. Her father signals her to come close, to bend forward. She bends close and leans her ear towards him. I cut to the outer room where her fiancé is asleep and Bhootnath is pacing. The scene in the outer room is lit by candlelight, and there is a lone candle burning steadily.

I wanted day to dawn as the scene progressed. I wanted Bhootnath to put out the candle so as to show up the light of dawn overshadowing the room. The effect I was aiming at was one of gloom. When the light outside gets brighter than the light inside, the light inside seems gloomy and in turn affects those in the room.

I told the lighting assistants to make the windows bright with whatever lights they wanted, so that there was an aura of gloom in the outer room when Jaba enters. She would enter, wake up her fiancé and tell him, 'Go home, and don't ever return.' He would get up and go. Bhootnath would then say, 'What happened?' At that point, Jaba is holding the back of a chair. I would track on to her knuckles, and then tilt up to her face, her set jaw, the strained neck muscles and then she would say, 'Come to the other room—father is dead.'

This was the shot I wanted. I told Murthy to place the camera on a low, three-inch stool, and tilt it up as the shot goes into close-up. Guru Dutt did not agree with the shot. He wanted the camera at eye level. I said, 'But I am imagining it in a particular way!'

He said, 'It's much too complicated, there is too much lighting.'

So, finally, we shot it with the camera at eye level. This was probably the first shot and so I agreed. But I did not quite give up. I asked for one more shot for my personal enlightenment and understanding. 'You keep this shot for editing,' I told Guru Dutt, 'but let me shoot it my way for my own knowledge.'

We completed that shot, and when we saw the rushes, he said, 'When challenged, you are right. I am sorry. Keep your shot at the time of editing.'

~

After that Guru Dutt left Abrar to his decisions and shot-taking, and did not interfere with his mode of direction. But Abrar was not completely happy with the lighting effects. 'I told Guru Dutt that Murthy had not quite given me what I wanted.'

Abrar's directorial responsibilities included, apart from deciding on the shot divisions, directing the actors through their dialogues and their characterizations—tasks he used to be involved with in his capacity as writer in the films that Guru Dutt directed. 'I had to manage each of the actors differently. They were all experienced hands, and I was a new director but I was very clear about what I wanted, and found ways of making each of the actors deliver,' he says.

19

Kuch Kah Na Sake
Uljhan Mein

After the first shooting schedule for *Sahib Bibi Aur Ghulam* was over, with the Waheeda sequences canned, Abrar set off to prepare for the location shooting for the rest of the movie. Most of the shooting till now had taken place on sets in Bombay, and there was a need for long shots and atmospheric shots to provide the background to the action, and locate the film in the right place and the right period.

When Guru Dutt had planned to direct the film himself, he had gone on a location hunt to Bengal, where he preferred to place most of his films. In this case, with the story being originally set in Bengal, it was only natural that he should seek locations in that state. Bimal Mitra had helped in his own way by introducing him to the play version of the novel and taking him around to acquaint him with various aspects of life that would help him create the right ambience for his film. The distributors of Guru Dutt Films in Bengal, Manna Ladda and Surju Ladda, enthusiastically took upon themselves the task of helping Guru Dutt find the right setting. After searching for locations, Guru Dutt had decided on a place called Dhanporia, forty miles out of Calcutta, just five miles away from the border of what was then East Pakistan (now Bangladesh).

The village was ideal, because it had an old haveli, rundown but still occupied, therefore, not in complete ruins, and Guru Dutt had decided that the family of Chhoti Bahu would be placed in this setting. The family that resided in the haveli was told that in return for letting the unit shoot on their property, the unit would restore the place.

Abrar flew to Calcutta, where he set up camp in Grand Hotel. It was to be his home for more than a month. The contractors that Abrar hired on behalf of Guru Dutt Films set about reconstructing the broken-down sections of the haveli and even constructing some portions that the visualization and story required. There was no electricity in the haveli, and with the help of the Laddas, the electricity department was persuaded to give enough power lines to enable shooting.

My only job in the first few days was to motor down every morning from Calcutta to Dhanporia and start putting the place in order, to ready it for the shoot. We got pumps set up and tube wells dug, for water. We plastered the walls and painted them again, we built the rooms that Bhootnath and his brother-in-law would live in; you can see all of it in the movie, as Bhootnath climbs up the stairs to his living quarters. It was all built for the film.

We built a makeshift fountain in front of the haveli, which is seen in the horse and carriage scenes. We had to build grandeur out of ruins. It looked like the work would never end. There was so much to do, and everything we touched seemed to need more detailed work than was evident at first sight.

Meanwhile, the unit in Bombay was getting restless. The producer could or would wait no longer. He kept pressurizing me to complete the set quickly, and I kept telling him I needed more time. Suddenly, one morning the entire unit landed in Calcutta. I was aghast, there was no way we could start shooting; the construction work was still under way, the place was not only not ready, it was in a total mess! The unit members lodged at Grand Hotel and twiddled their thumbs, while I ferried up and down, urging the contractors to hurry and get the haveli ready in time.

I had been allotted a twenty-day schedule for shooting all the haveli scenes. By the time the setting was ready, I had only ten days in hand. The unit members could not extend their stay, they had commitments back in Bombay, so I ended up shooting all the location sequences back to back, round the clock.

Shooting also involved getting horses from Calcutta, procuring carriages, laying down trolley tracks, and finding a lot of new angles to the lighting, something that had Abrar at his wits' end more often than not. The night scenes in particular taxed Abrar's capabilities. He worked out a way to make up for the shortage of time by making the most of the available light. But as a first-time director, there were instances when in visualizing a scene he would lose sight of the practical difficulties that could crop up while shooting. Like the time when he wanted to show the entire haveli in a long shot with Sapru standing at the top of the stairs.

I visualized a shot clearly enough, but did not always take in the practical difficulties that could arise while shooting it. In this particular instance, I had planned the scene and set the camera accordingly only to discover that the lighting fell short. There was no light on

Sapru's face. I wondered how I could solve this, as placing extra lights to light up his face would mean having them within the frame. Murthy and I taxed our brains on how to solve the problem. I finally thought it out and placed baby lights on the pillars of the haveli, on the side that was behind the camera. The shot was taken.

I reorganized the shooting schedule according to the lighting, rather than working in sequence. So I would shoot the morning scenes first, then as the sun went overhead, I would shoot the scenes set at that time, and then move to the evening scenes at dusk. That way I could keep the continuity and yet save time.

Shooting would end by two a.m., and we would pack up by three-thirty a.m. or so, and the next schedule would start at six a.m.! It meant a lot of homework, but in the process I gained a lot of confidence. After this ten-day shooting stint I knew I could handle any situation as a director.

We would go to Calcutta once in two or three days and watch the rushes in the projection room we had hired there. I told Guru Dutt, 'Please check out the scene and the rushes, I am tired and very involved in shooting and given the tight schedule I do not think I can afford to drive up and down and waste so much time.' He took on the job willingly.

When he saw the scene of Sapru in long shot in the haveli, he was full of praise for the lighting. He told Murthy that the lighting was nothing short of genius. I heard from Guru Dutt himself that Murthy gave me the full credit for the lighting of that scene. As for me, I feel I had just followed the advice Guru Dutt had given me when I started shooting for the film. He told me two things. One was to shoot with the third eye that I possessed as the man who had written and recorded the entire film. And the second was to ignore Murthy's laments. He said, '*Murthy ki bilkul nahin sunna, bahut kun-kun karega*, but direct him properly and he delivers the goods.'

Guru Dutt, as always, played an avuncular role, inculcating a family feeling among the members of the unit, ensuring that despite the stressful conditions everyone worked as a close-knit team. There were fights and arguments, Abrar remembers, with unit members even calling each other names in the heat of the moment, but they stuck together and gave their best for a common cause, the project. Yet, despite all the family feeling, Abrar had his first serious scrap with the unit during the shooting schedule at Dhanporia. One evening, he was waiting to shoot a sequence while the rest of the unit, Guru Dutt included, were on the terrace having a drink and enjoying jokes. Abrar got angry enough to walk up the stairs and lash at them for being unprofessional.

❧

It was the peak of summer, a hot sweaty day in May, and the work was unending and very taxing for everyone concerned. More often than not, stress levels were high and we were all on a short fuse. I am like a man possessed when I work. Guru Dutt was different in temperament, he kept his equanimity. Nothing fazed him. I, on the other hand, am more hot-tempered and cannot brook distractions. 'I am almost dead with exhaustion and overwork,' I shouted, 'and none of you are professional enough to even come on time for a shot . . .'

Some of the others were visibly upset over my outburst. They felt it was unpardonable that I should shout thus, especially since Guru Dutt was part of the group. But Guru Dutt, after a momentary silence, took charge of the situation, and broke up the gathering, so that shooting could resume.

Later, Abrar would once again find himself flouting the norms of common politeness and public relations, immersed as he was in his work. It was while he was rehearsing Meena Kumari for a shot in Bombay. The two star actors of the era, Raj Kapoor and Rajendra Kumar, walked in to visit the actress, who had been their co-star in many films. Common courtesy demanded that the director welcome them, offer them hospitality and spend some time in polite conversation. But Abrar, engrossed in his work, did none of this. He continued to rehearse his actress, and once rehearsal was done with, proceeded to shoot.

The common practice I followed throughout the film was to get two okay takes, so we went through six or seven takes before the scene ended and I called cut for the final time. I knew that Raj Kapoor and Rajendra Kumar were on the catwalk above the set, leaning on the overhead railing, watching me. But before I could finish, they left, turning down the offer of tea a unit hand had made.

When the scene was over, Meena Kumari came to me and asked very sweetly if she had my permission to speak to her guests. I said, 'Fine, it will take me about two hours to light the next scene, so you can go and meet them.' I did not realize at the time that she was being sarcastic, or that everyone had been shocked at the way I had ignored two of the industry's biggest personalities. It was only a day later that this fact hit home.

Lekh Tandon was directing *Professor* at the same time that I was working on *Sahib Bibi Aur Ghulam*. As I was also involved with *Professor* as its writer, we would meet every few days. He told me, 'You have insulted my guru,' meaning Raj Kapoor, who was close to him. 'You did not even ask him what he wanted.' I replied that it was only because I was engrossed in my work, shooting. 'But he felt insulted,' Lekh continued, 'he told bhabhi [Krishna Kapoor] about it and she told me.'

I told Lekh that that was never my intention. Raj and Rajendra are important pillars of the film industry, I said, why would I want to insult them? Rajendra Kumar was also a good friend of mine, I had shared a room with him during shooting in the past. I said to Lekh, 'Let's go to Rajendra Kumar's house and see how we can solve this misunderstanding.'

When Rajendra Kumar also confirmed that Raj had felt insulted, and had remarked that while most people fawn over him, I had not even looked in his direction, I replied that I was made that way. 'You know me,' I said, 'even if God comes down when I am shooting I cannot let go of my work.'

I met Raj Kapoor later and apologized for the unmeant affront, telling him that both Lekh and Rajendra Kumar had reported that he had felt I had belittled him. But he said, 'I have no complaints.' 'If you really mean what you say, come to the premiere of my film,' I told him. Raj Kapoor promised to come, but he never did.

20

Main Toh Tann Mann Ki
Sudh Budh Gava . . .

Looking back at *Sahib Bibi Aur Ghulam*, Abrar is today justifiably proud of having made a film that called upon the last reserves of his creative energies and challenged him to give his best. But at that time, when he had just agreed, albeit a bit reluctantly, to take on the direction of the film, he did not realize how much it would demand of him.

The issues that faced him were manifold and kept coming up like waves against the shore, even as the film progressed. Casting was among the first. The task of signing on and directing an artist of the stature of Meena Kumari was a formidable one for the first-time director, even with the Guru Dutt Films banner backing him. Then there was the fact that he had a handful of high-profile actors to manage, very different from one another in temperament and their approach to acting and, finally, there was his producer and boss, Guru Dutt, to contend with as the main actor.

These would have been enough to make any director work overtime, but there was the additional factor that Guru Dutt, despite inviting his writer to handle the directorial reins, was often enthused to step in and try and make things go his way. That he finally shot the song sequences himself is the primary reason why a considerable part of the cinema world believes to this day that he was the real hand behind the film, and Abrar only a shadow director.

But despite many skirmishes and one particularly nasty one where Abrar almost threw in the reins and stomped out of the film, the fact remains that in their own way the two men brought to *Sahib Bibi Aur Ghulam* enough intensity and talent to make it an all-time classic. If today, four decades after the film stormed the public consciousness, Abrar is still faced with the question of whether he was only a ghost director, he is justified in feeling bitter about it. There are enough witnesses still alive to prove that Abrar was indeed the main architect of the classic, and in his own memory there are enough instances to vouch for his deep and complete involvement. And in that, there is much that enchants and entertains.

My problems with the film began with the casting of its central character—Chhoti Bahu. After deciding not to cast Chhaya Arya, Guru Dutt resolved that Meena Kumari would be good for the role. She was a saleable star and had the histrionic ability to take on the demanding role. However, Guru Dutt was chary of asking her husband Kamal Amrohi. Kamal was very possessive and was sure to quote a high price just to discourage too many offers coming in the way of his own work with his wife. So like in many other such tricky situations over the last few years, it fell upon me to help Guru Dutt get Meena through some other means.

Abrar went across to meet the actress, ensuring that she gave him enough time for him to play the entire spool of the recording. It worked. Meena Kumari was so entranced by the theme and the potential of the role of Chhoti Bahu that she decided she had to play the role. The rest was easy, as the actress took on the job of convincing her husband. Though the film went on the sets soon after this episode, it would still be a long wait before Meena Kumari would become Chhoti Bahu.

Almost an entire year after he first wielded the megaphone for *Sahib Bibi Aur Ghulam* would Abrar start shooting with Meena Kumari. Meena Kumari had agreed, rather insisted, that she would shoot her portions in one uninterrupted sequence, without breaks. This suited Abrar Alvi too, as it meant that he would be able to concentrate on her completely and she would, in turn, be able to give the film her undivided attention. But within the first three days of shooting with an actress who had a formidable reputation as a dedicated, beautiful and consummate artist, the director ran into trouble.

It was the very first scene where the audience would see Meena Kumari as Chhoti Bahu. Guru Dutt, playing Bhootnath, has been summarily summoned by Chhoti Bahu, and is meeting her with great trepidation. He has found his way around the haveli and stumbled into her room, walking in with much hesitation, awed by the ambience and the very fact of being in her presence.

He crouches, villager style, on the floor, his eyes focused on her feet. It is obvious she is seated. A soft and gentle voice asks him his name, and he says, 'Bhootnath.' He is used to most people laughing at the name, but is surprised to hear the owner of the soft and gentle voice tell him that she thinks it is a nice name. He looks up at her face, quite forgetting his shyness.

The shot included an empty bed, symbolic of her life, and other furniture that created the right ambience. But my shot-taking was falling short of my visualization. I kept changing the camera angle, then put the camera on trolley, yet it would not look the way I wanted it to look. Then I tried raising the camera. That did not work either. Both Murthy and I struggled with the scene for all of two hours without any luck or success.

Guru Dutt finally asked me what the matter was. 'You've taken two hours for this scene,' he said, 'what's wrong?'

I said, 'I really need a dolly; that is how I now visualize this scene.'

Guru Dutt said, 'Why didn't you tell me yesterday that you needed a dolly. We could have got it.'

I explained that to begin with I had visualized the scene differently, but now a dolly was intrinsic to my visualization and shot-taking. He did not waste a minute. He asked me to wait, and sent someone to Mohan Studios where Bimal Roy was shooting. They could borrow a dolly from there. But there was no dolly at Mohan Studios, and the schedule had to be stopped.

'We will shoot this scene after lunch,' Guru Dutt said. 'I will have the dolly procured from Dadar.' When I demurred, he said, 'We shall wait. Do not compromise on your scene.'

As particular of another's work as he was about his own, Guru Dutt ensured that Abrar shot the scene just the way he wanted to. All should have been well once the scene was shot as per Abrar's visualization, but there was more trouble ahead for the director.

The rushes came in the next day. And after seeing them I was horrified. Guru Dutt asked me, 'What happened, why are you so upset?' I replied, 'You have acted so well . . . lost in her beauty, you look exactly the way that someone who sees great beauty should look. Your expressions are perfect.' 'So, what's wrong,' he asked again.

I told him that earlier, Bansi, Bhootnath's kinsman, had described Chhoti Bahu with the words, '*Chand mein bhi daag hai, un mein nahin*', so the audience is expecting someone breathtaking to appear on screen. But Meena is looking awful!

Guru Dutt was perplexed and decided to check it out for himself. He came back after seeing the rushes, saying, 'Yes, there is something wrong. Let me see how to tackle this. Maybe Murthy needs to change the lighting or something.'

He advised me not to shoot the scene the next day, but to use the time to shoot a lot of still photographs of Meena Kumari, from all angles, getting enough long-shots and close-ups. 'Tell her it is for publicity,' he added, 'it will give us the time we need. And get the shots processed and printed as soon as possible.'

Guru Dutt read a lot, knew enough about cameras to take them apart and put them together again. He had an impressive collection of books, including technical books on cameras and photography. Photoflash delivered the prints the next morning. We reached the studio. Guru Dutt took out two thick books on photography with portions marked in pencil. He handed them to me. 'Read this,' he said.

That is how I understood the problem with my shots of Meena. At that time, the Mitchell camera used a 75mm lens for close-ups, while an 18mm lens was used for natural shots, as were 20, 45 and 50mm lenses. The book explained that the 75mm lens broadens a subject in close-up while an 18mm elongates the same subject. Meena Kumari's face was broad, and she had the habit of lifting her face when delivering dialogues to the camera. I discussed the matter with Guru Dutt. I said, 'According to the book, a 75mm lens will broaden her face further, but that is the favoured close-up lens for most cameramen. Meena Kumari's face should be taken in close-up with a lens of lower density.'

Guru Dutt explained that cameramen use the 75mm lens for their own convenience, because it can be kept at a distance from the subject. The camera being heavy then does not need to be moved for close-up shots. Also, shooting from far, there is more scope for strong lighting, and no improvisation is called for. A close camera meant lesser scope for strong lighting, it demanded technical thought, and nuances had to be worked into the lighting for it to be effective. Murthy had not expended any thought on shooting Meena Kumari's face to advantage. I decided to shoot with a 40mm lens, except in one scene where I used a 50mm lens.

All the stills had been taken in profile or in three-fourth angle. We studied the stills and retouched them for the publicity release. In the process we realized that Meena Kumari's face looked good in profile from one side and in three-fourth angle from the other. We decided that we would shoot Chhoti Bahu only in profile and three-fourth face, except for one scene.

This decision to shoot only from angles demanded great deliberation before shot-taking. Other aspects of his decision to shoot no full frontals of Meena's face had also to be considered. The scene where Chhoti Bahu wears the Mohini Sindoor for the first time, for example, was particularly tricky. The scene shows her wearing a large tikka of the Mohini Sindoor on her forehead. She calls to her husband, '*Ek baar idhar dekho na ...*' It had to be shot differently if Abrar wanted to avoid a head-on shot. Abrar explains the mechanics of how he handled the scene.

Her husband (Rehman) is looking at his wrist, tying a garland around it. I had the camera track forward and run so close that only her forehead could be seen, and the tikka and the nose. Her eyes were bound to blink during the shot, so I used the 50mm lens and shot as if she was being seen through her husband's eyes. Thus I moved from a full long-shot to a close-up, with a cut to Rehman.

I had to remember where to place the camera to go with our decision of shooting Meena Kumari only in profile and three-fourth face. I had to remember which side to shoot to get the best profile and where to place the camera for the three-fourth angle. Then, all movements and characters had to be orchestrated accordingly.

I enlisted Meena's help to prompt me, 'This is for my profile, and this side is for the three-fourth shots.' Before the shot, I would say, profile, and she would point to the correct side, and if I said three-fourth, she would indicate which side of her face needed to be shot. That was a code we worked out, so I knew where to place the camera.

Mala Sinha visited the sets quite frequently; she was a close friend of Meena's, and she would wonder what was happening. She guessed something was up, but could never really make out that it was our secret code to get Meena Kumari's best angles. Finally, after a few shots, Meena told me, 'The nose ring side is the profile side while the side without the nose ring is for the three-fourth angle shots.'

It was in the same Mohini Sindoor scene that Abrar tried another experiment with shot-taking. The scene begins with Chhoti Bahu telling Bansi, 'Make any excuse but send my husband to my room.' She has placed a big tikka of Mohini Sindoor on her forehead and some more in the parting of her hair. Rehman comes in, a garland around his wrist, twiddling with the threads, trying to tie the garland. Chhoti Bahu tells him to look at her, he does, and the camera gives us a close-up of the sindoor in the parting of her hair. He says, 'I have no time for such rubbish.' He moves, crosses the room, she follows and holds on to his shoulder. 'You go every day,' she tells him, 'why not stay with me today?' He asks her, 'Can you keep a man of the Chaudhuri khandan happy?'

∽

I could have had her at his feet beseeching him to stay, but I made her come close to him and rest against his shoulder, to suggest her sexuality. I show her lips come close, and he holds her shoulder and asks, 'Can you do this, can you drink?'

She moves back in shock, the trolley moves towards her and continues as she starts approaching the trolley. Never before in Guru Dutt Films had such a reverse shot been taken. Murthy was taken aback. He said, 'What are you doing, such a shot has never been taken in Guru Dutt Films.' I told him, 'The history of Guru Dutt Films is not over yet, it is being made, take the shot.'

'Where will the trolley stop?' Murthy wanted to know.

I told him to cut at the climax of 'will you drink with me'.

The shot following this one showed Meena's face and Rehman's back on trolley movement. It was a signature scene that marked the film as mine. Such shot-taking had not been seen in any other film of Guru Dutt's from *Baazi* to *Kaagaz Ke Phool*.

∽

Though Abrar Alvi has no qualms in acknowledging the debt he owes Guru Dutt for the confidence he reposed in Abrar's directorial abilities and for the freedom he allowed his director in running the show of *Sahib Bibi Aur Ghulam* from day one, there was one aspect of the film Guru Dutt could not let go of: he could not bring himself to let the songs be directed by anyone else. Guru Dutt's desire to shoot the songs of the film that he had asked Abrar Alvi to direct was so overpowering that Abrar had no option but to acquiesce. If this rankles with Abrar he does not show it, but is magnanimous enough to admit that when it came to song picturization, there was no one quite like Guru Dutt.

There are very few directors with such a strong sense of mood and mastery over the medium, and I must have learnt a lot about directing a film watching him and working as his assistant. When it came to picturizing songs, he had almost no equal. It was something he was passionate about and did exceedingly well.

Right at the beginning, I had shot the song '*Bhanwara bada nadaan hai*' on Waheeda. I had wanted to show the Brahmo Samaj background she belonged to, and as the Brahmo Samaj manners were westernized to a degree, I had given her clothes that hinted at this, and made her work on a painting that was also Western in its lines. I requested Guru Dutt's sister, the artist Lalitha Lajmi, to help me with the scene. I wanted to show the audience the painting that Waheeda was working on, and got Lalitha to do one for me, and shot Lalitha's hand drawing some of the lines, but Guru Dutt would have none of it.

He was unable to accept the fact that someone else was shooting the songs in his production. He found an excuse to send me off. He sent me location hunting to Bengal, and while I was away, re-shot the entire song sequence. The painting and Lalitha Lajmi's hand were all done away with. However, the song still works wonderfully as a scene.

I remember Guruswamy coming up to me when I was preparing to shoot the song '*Na jao saiyan*', and hinting that Guru Dutt wanted to be present. 'Everyone says Guru Dutt is the master of song picturization, why not let him come on the sets?' he asked.

I replied that any scene and even a song was the interpretation of an individual. 'Either he does it or I do it,' I said. Guru Dutt had already reworked a song sequence I had shot on Waheeda, and I knew what he was up to. I told Guruswamy, 'He is the producer, he has every right to shoot the songs if that is what he wants to do. Please tell him to go right ahead.'

However, I did not want to be present at the time of the shoot. It was not right to have two directors on one set, and so I left the floor to my producer. I briefed Murthy though, telling him that the camera should not leave the bed on which Meena Kumari lay—the bed was symbolic of her loneliness and empty sexual life, and should be the focal point of her song.

Guru Dutt took over from my first shot. When the song was to end, he sent his assistant to me. 'Guru Dutt says he will complete his picturization of the song today, and there is no break after it for the next scene. He wants you to indicate how you want to take it forward, so he can finish it in a way that will suit you,' he said.

I told him, 'Tell him to finish it as he pleases. I will take it forward.'

The shooting of the song was completed only the next day. Just before that his assistant came to me again. 'There is still time,' he said, 'tell us how you want him to end the song.'

I refused. 'Tell me when the last shot is done, I will come,' I said.

When I was told the last shot was over, I went to the sets. I did not know how Guru Dutt had finished the song. I asked the cameraman's assistant, Prabhakar, how the shot had been taken. He said, 'Rehman is standing and Meena is sitting at his feet. She had fallen to his feet at the line "*tumhare charnon mein aa gayi hoon*".'

I asked him why the scene had shifted from the bed, which is the way I had wanted the song to end. He said till the last shot it was all shot on the bed but . . .

I asked him, 'Was Rehman wearing shoes, or was he barefoot?'

Prabhakar said his feet were bare. I got his shoes put at the farthest corner.

I said, 'Let's not wait.'

I knew that Murthy could take ages to light a scene. Give him a change of lighting at this point and the scene would not be shot within that schedule.

I said, 'Let Rehman walk from there, move the camera up from his feet as he puts on his shoes, then move up to full figure, let him turn and say his dialogue: "*Kya nayi baat kah rahi ho tum.*" And then pack-up.'

I then spent the night with my viewfinder doing the shot division, and today challenge anyone to prove that there were two people who worked on that scene.

There was another reason why I stayed away from the song sequences. Early on in the shooting, I had told Guru Dutt that I did not want him to be present in any of the scenes between Meena Kumari and Rehman, unless his presence was required as an artist. 'You will crack jokes and distract the actors and it is a serious film and I want no distractions,' I had told him, and he had respected that. Thus, on my part, I had no choice but to keep away when he was directing the songs.

∼

As such, the only song Abrar was allowed to shoot was the atmospheric '*Koi door se awaaz de*'. However, even if song sequences were out of his reach, Abrar still had the expression of the actors to deal with, and that, as he claims, was his forte. He had to work with each actor differently, as each one of them was an established name and had a style of his or her own. Listening to him one gets an idea about his methods of rehearsing artists for a shot. His inability to direct Waheeda as he would have wished to has been mentioned earlier, but Abrar had his hands full with Guru Dutt himself. To make an actor who carried an image of a suave and polished man of the world acceptable as a country bumpkin was no mean task, and if Abrar is to be believed, Guru Dutt was not a man with great histrionic abilities.

I had to teach him how to appear foolish and intimidated. I dressed him in such a way—high dhoti, squeaky shoes—that the appearance spoke of his rural roots, and gave him mannerisms that would accentuate the background. In fact, I even indicated through cues the pauses during the delivery of a line of dialogue to get the desired effect.

I had done so even in *Kaagaz Ke Phool*, for example, in the scene where Guru Dutt delivers the line in response to the accusation by his producers that he is a spent force. He says, 'I am not a flop director, I am just . . .' Here I asked him to pause, hold his breath and then sigh as he said the words 'very tired'.

Similarly, in *Sahib Bibi Aur Ghulam*, I had to actually add pauses, an accent and mannerisms to make the character come alive on screen. Of course as the film progresses, refinement comes in and he becomes more of a city man and less of a country bumpkin.

Meena Kumari was quite another story. She had listened to the tape a number of times and could get into the mood of the character and the dialogues. But I had to rehearse her to take her to the pitch I required and then let her take the scene forward on her own.

I don't think highly of directors who resort to formulaic methods of rehearsing an actor. The personality and background of the artist matter; in some cases you must be soft, in others loud or hard. A histrionic director's job is to inspire the artist to the right pitch, so as to deliver the perfect performance, and that includes the pitch of voice. I used to handle Meena Kumari and Rehman very differently.

I could see in Meena's eyes whether inwardly she had risen to the desired, correct pitch. The way to ensure she got to that state was to work myself up to that pitch so she could see herself in me, and then rise to that level. To extract that from her, I had to burn a lot of my energy. I would tell her, 'Let your voice reach the heavens . . .' and she would take it from there. I would rehearse the scene and explain it first, then work it as close to the real thing as possible so that Meena Kumari could give exactly what was wanted of her. Then, before we started shooting, I would signal to the cameraman and instruct the sound man to keep the sound rolling. I added that there would be no clap between takes, the pace would be as near to real life as possible. The takes would follow seamlessly if needed, and the clap would come in only at the end of the okay take.

In every tense scene I would tell Guru Dutt to keep away from the sets, no outsider was allowed, so that the tension could be maintained. After hearing a dramatic scene, Meena would often request that we hold on to the momentum and that the serious atmosphere that had developed during the rehearsal prevail on the set. Guru Dutt had the habit of joking around, and he being the boss I knew I had no power to stop him, so the best way was to keep him off the sets, in deference to Meena's request. Of course, Guru Dutt didn't like being told to keep off the sets of his own production, but he respected me as the director, and kept away.

❧

All of a sudden, Abrar changes gears as he narrates this and, shrugging his shoulders as if to get into the past, recites a dialogue: '*Hindu ghar ki bahu hoke sharaab pi hai kisine?*' His voice is loud and high-pitched, and there is an uncanny feeling that someone has switched on the television set in the room. Just as suddenly, he comes back to the present and to being himself.

Yet, he says, there were times when Meena was unhappy with her own interpretation of a particular scene. Abrar tells of the time when Meena Kumari was dubbing for the scene when she meets Bhootnath for the first time. She is a woman who has no malice, her voice had to brim over with motherly love, and she had to let the dialogue portray her loving nature.

She worked on the scene, we did two takes, but my assistant Raj Kumar Bedi wasn't happy. '*Baat nahin ban rahi*,' he said. I said, 'It's okay, leave it, let it be ...' But Meena Kumari was not satisfied either. She insisted on knowing what was wrong. Bedi said, 'It's not like what Abrar said on tape.' She called for the tape and listened to it. She got up in great anger and smashed her fist on the wall, asking, 'Why can't I speak like that?'

I thought it was time to intervene. I said, 'You need to be born again to be able to speak like I did.' She looked at me askance, probably offended. I explained, 'Your voice lacks the bass of a man's voice, so it is best as you said it. It cannot get better in a woman's voice. When you go into the "tadap" scenes, where you suffer and agonize—that is a woman's forte—I won't be able to do it as well as you, and you will far surpass the tape. Each voice has its own peculiarities.'

Then there was the scene in which Meena Kumari has to fall down. I told her I want you to fall like a cut tree. Of course it was not easy to understand what exactly I wanted, and Meena being the perfectionist she was, wanted to know exactly what I meant. Communicating it in words was inadequate, so I decided to demonstrate. I crashed to the floor and in the process hit my head on some furniture and got a huge bump on my head. Anyway, Meena got the idea pretty well and worked the scene out wonderfully. A bit too wonderfully, in fact, going by what happened after the shot was completed.

She had got under the skin of the scene and ended up crying. Even after the scene was over, she continued to cry uncontrollably, and seemed to be quite inconsolable. Shyam, another of my assistants, came up to me and said, 'Please go and console her, we do not know how to make her stop.'

I had never touched a 'gair' woman before. After all, I came from an orthodox Muslim family, but now I realized that I had to put my qualms aside. I put out my hand and held Meena by the shoulder, and finally she emerged out of the scene.

Perhaps it was the deep involvement in her role as Chhoti Bahu and the results she saw on screen that made Meena Kumari say later, 'Abrar draws out the best in me!' Abrar, in turn, as much as the public which watched *Sahib Bibi Aur Ghulam*, was impressed by Meena Kumari's talent, dedication and the way she approached the role. He had worked with her earlier, but hadn't seen anything extraordinary. But with *Sahib Bibi Aur Ghulam*, Abrar realized that Meena Kumari was an artist capable of rising to great histrionic heights, if the role demanded it.

I must admit that at the beginning I wondered why such a fuss was made over the actress. People spoke the name 'Meenaji' with such awe, but though I had worked with her in two films, I had never seen that flash of legendary talent. She had not been given a chance in most films. It was her status as a saleable star that was being exploited and she was almost running from one set to the next and going through her roles mechanically. Yes, her statement about my ability to draw out the best in her remains one of the proudest moments of my cinematic journey. There is no record of this statement, unfortunately. But I know for sure that she was so immersed in the role through the weeks of shooting that at some point the despair and depression of Chhoti Bahu must have affected her peace of mind.

∽

Sure enough, in Meena Kumari's diary there is an entry which reads, 'I am sick to death of Chhoti Bahu.'

Abrar handled Rehman and Sapru quite differently as well. Unlike Guru Dutt, these two were consummate actors who did not need to be closely directed. But unlike Meena Kumari, they were not stars; rather they were accomplished character actors and as such Abrar's approach was markedly different with them. With Rehman in particular there was a certain camaraderie which influenced their on-set relationship.

∽

I used to call him Pathan and we went on to become quite close friends. The relationship between Rehman and me was more man to man. This particular scene had him lying in bed, his lower body covered with a shawl; it is soon after he has been afflicted by a stroke. I had just finished a scene with Meena and was quite hyper and worked up after creating the mood for her. I went up to Rehman as he lay waiting for his shot and, placing my hand on his thigh, started explaining the scene to him. Under normal circumstances, it was usually enough to give him the scene and the background and ask for the emotion required, but in the mood I was at that moment, I got carried away and continued to tell him, in great detail, what was expected of him.

Finally, exhausted from the detailing, I took a deep breath and asked him, 'Did you understand, Pathan?' and he shouted back, 'I will, baba, but how can I concentrate on what you are saying if you do not stop kneading my thigh.'

Handling Sapru was quite another matter though. He was a seasoned actor, and had fixed views on his method of delivering dialogues. Sapru believed that expression was controlled by breath, a laudable and worthy idea, except for the fact that he had a rather pronounced belly that would bounce around with his deep breaths.

I was worried that his dialogue style would diminish his presence on screen. I had to find a way of ensuring that the character of Sapru remained a larger-than-life one. After all, Sapru played the master of the haveli, the elder brother who ruled over the zamindari, the haveli and was the keeper of its 'morality', despite his own wanton ways.

I did away with a lot of Sapru's dialogues. I trimmed his scenes and ensured that his lackeys spoke on his behalf. Needless to say, Sapru was distraught, but I reassured him. I told him that by speaking little and looking imposing and regal, he would come across as a sinister personality whose very appearance on screen would inform the audience that there was trouble ahead.

When I wanted him to order the murder of Chhoti Bahu, I had the lackeys, hefty men who looked like executioners, come up to him and say, '*Hathiyaron ko zung lag gayi hai, sarkar,*' and had him take off his ring and hand it to them. The effect of that scene is chilling and marks his personality in no uncertain manner.

I told Sapru, 'Sapru Sahab, you will score, your character will remain memorable, I am approaching it differently.' And to my credit, it worked wonderfully well.

∼

This brings Abrar to the one aspect of the film which still rankles with him after all these years: the impression that his directorial credit is merely a façade for Guru Dutt. He is emphatic about *Sahib Bibi Aur Ghulam* being his work in every respect. Apart from the number of witnesses to the fact, there is one piece of evidence from Guru Dutt himself which proves this beyond an iota of doubt. Interestingly enough, this indisputable proof came about thanks to Abrar's decision to give up the film and leave Guru Dutt Films during the making of *Sahib Bibi Aur Ghulam*.

∼

There are witnesses to the fact that we directed our scenes individually. Guru Dutt was involved only with the song sequences. Atma Ram's wife, Veena, asked me many times over why Guru Dutt was being kept away from the sets. He was after all the owner and the master and the producer. On the last day of shooting, he came on the sets, and when Meena Kumari asked him why he had stayed away all these days, he laughed and responded, 'I was obeying my director's orders!'

Coming to my decision to resign from Guru Dutt Films—it was a strange situation. For perhaps the only time in our relationship, Guru Dutt lost his temper with me. We were shooting a difficult scene, Rehman is in bed, paralysed, and I had shot it in a way that neither Y.G. Chavan, the editor, nor Guru Dutt could make sense of. There were shots of flying leaves interspersed.

The editor asked me, 'How do I cut this scene? I cannot understand it. Is there some mistake?' I said, 'No, there is no mistake.' He went back to the editing room, tried his hand at editing the scene and came back again. I lost my cool and said, 'Leave me alone, let me shoot.'

He must have gone and complained to Guru Dutt, because soon enough Guru Dutt's man, Ratan, was standing at my elbow, saying, 'Sahab wants you, come at once.'

From his tone I knew there was trouble ahead. I went to the first floor where Guru Dutt had his office, and entered the room. He started shouting at me almost immediately: 'Who do you think you are? Is it your film? It is *my* film.'

I waited till he calmed down and told him, 'If Chavan had told me that you wanted an explanation of the way I have visualized and shot the scene, I would have stopped my work and come. I thought he felt something was wrong with the scene and was not prepared to wait for me to clear it up.'

I left the room, went back to my place and wrote a letter to him, telling him it was his film, and that I did not want to be part of it. 'Do what you want with the movie,' I wrote. 'I want no credit—I have nothing to do with the film.' I dropped the letter off at his house at about five p.m.

He wrote me a reply: 'You have directed the movie, the credit is yours, and the discredit, if any, is yours.' I still have that precious letter with me and it is the irrefutable proof, to all those who claim that my name was merely a front for Guru Dutt, that I was indeed the director of *Sahib Bibi Aur Ghulam.*

21

Naache Jiya Ghoom Ke

Sahib Bibi Aur Ghulam was a bigger hit than all of Guru Dutt's earlier films. The combined geniuses of Guru Dutt and Abrar Alvi ensured that every aspect of the film was technically sound and emotionally powerful. It went on to win a number of awards, including the Filmfare Award for Best Film, the Filmfare Critics' Award, and the President's Award for Best Feature Film in Hindi.

In March 1963, Guru Dutt and Abrar went to Delhi to receive the Silver Lotus from the then President of India, Dr S. Radhakrishnan. Meena Kumari accompanied them along with her husband, Kamal Amrohi, who was loath to let her travel alone anywhere. While the producer and director stayed at the Ashoka Hotel, Meena and Kamal Amrohi stayed with the mayor of Delhi, as his guests.

The mayor arranged a reception for Meena Kumari which was attended by the minister for information and broadcasting and other dignitaries, including the maharaja of Baroda, and director C.V. Sridhar who was to receive an award for the Best Film in Tamil. Abrar met Sridhar for the first time that evening and they went on to become good friends.

The next day, they all met again, at the awards function where Meena Kumari sat next to Abrar. Guru Dutt sat further down the same row. It was a time to feel proud of belonging to Guru Dutt Films. And of their own achievements. The three representatives were justifiably happy with their moment in the limelight.

~

We each have a memento of the award—mine still stands on the counterpane in my room. I remember it was at the function that Meena told me, 'We will go farther than Delhi with this film.' I asked her where and she answered, 'Berlin. Wait and watch, we will go to Berlin.' She informed me that our film had been nominated to the Berlin Film Festival. I asked her how she knew of this, and she smiled and said, 'Don't you know with whom I am staying? I have the information and it's pucca.' That was the first time I heard of *Sahib Bibi Aur Ghulam* going to Berlin as the official entry of the Government of India.

Once the ceremony was over, Meena Kumari left with her husband, while we made our way back to the hotel. We were in the car when Guru Dutt asked me, 'What next, Abrar?'

Sahib Bibi Aur Ghulam had been released ten months ago, and true to form Guru Gutt had not been quiet in the interim. He was already planning his next project. He informed me that he had made all arrangements to get the rights for *President*, which had been a hit film in the 1930s, with K.L. Saigal and Leela Desai playing the lead roles. 'I want you to direct it,' he told me.

I said nothing. But I was upset. *President* was a big drop, it would be a let-down after *Sahib Bibi Aur Ghulam*, which was already being spoken of as a classic and had done wonderfully well even in a city like Bombay.

I told him I would not direct *President*. I was just not inspired by the story. He insisted and said, 'Think it over.' I told him, 'I have a story I want to make.' He was curious and said, 'Let me hear it.'

I said, 'I want to make Premchand's "Kafan". That is the film I really feel inspired to direct.'

Guru Dutt could drip sarcasm if he chose to. 'Who do you think you are, Satyajit Ray?' he asked. I held on to my choice, countering that aspiring to be Ray was not such a bad thing after all. But he would not let the matter rest. He worried the issue like a dog worries a rag. 'It's a morbid theme, it has a morbid title, with negative characters. Who will see it?' he mused.

The conversation did not get any further, as the twosome had to make arrangements to go to Berlin in June—the film was to be screened on 26 June. Guru Dutt had an additional agenda for his trip to Berlin. He hoped to use the visit to get his teeth attended to. He had had his crooked front teeth removed and wanted to have implants put in. Someone had told him that Berlin was the ideal place for implants; the experts were to be found there. And Guru Dutt had been in correspondence with a dental house for a while, setting up an appointment. He decided that as soon as the demands of the film festival were over, he would get his teeth fixed. The dates were duly given to him from Berlin; it would need about two weeks for the dental work to be completed, and thus he would remain in Berlin till the middle of July.

The film festival spanned twelve days, which meant that if Guru Dutt attended the festival from the beginning to the end, he would be away from India for almost an entire month. He could not afford to stay away for such a long while, so he decided to come to Berlin on a date closer to the screening of his film. Waheeda was part of the delegation too, and Abrar and Waheeda left first, to be present at the start of the festival.

Much drama surrounded the trip that the delegation from Guru Dutt Films made to the Berlin Film Festival.

❦

We were all booked to go by Air India. Waheeda, Waheeda's sister, Sayeeda, and I were travelling together. Also with us was J.K. Kapoor, brother of my old nemesis K.K. Kapoor and the public relations officer for Guru Dutt Films. Guru Dutt would follow later. V. Shantaram, a member of the Berlin jury panel, was also to travel with us. The flight was booked to enable us to reach in time for the inauguration.

We arrived at the airport and were waiting for Shantaram. So imagine our surprise when we saw B.R. Chopra instead. He told us that V. Shantaram had fallen sick. BR was still at his office that evening when he got a call to replace V. Shantaram. There was, however, a condition: he had to leave the same night and board the flight we were boarding!

Chopra had always been a man of quick decisions and prompt action. He said, 'I will make it.' He phoned his house and asked for a suit to be sent across to his office so that he could go straight to the airport and make it to the flight on time. And just as well. He was great company and very resourceful.

❦

Abrar got quite close to B.R. Chopra during their trip to Berlin. However, the same was not the case with the relationship between B.R. Chopra and Guru Dutt. BR was a successful producer with hit films like *Naya Daur*, *Dhool Ka Phool* and *Gumrah* under his belt, while Guru Dutt was also a hero with a nice smile and a sensitive face besides being a producer and director. As Abrar remembers it, the rivalry was marked from B.R. Chopra's side, though Guru Dutt never let anyone know how he felt about BR. They were civil to one another, but considered themselves rivals.

Before Guru Dutt arrived in Berlin, B.R. Chopra would go over and chat with Abrar whenever he got the chance, despite the fact that he was on the jury and Abrar was only a delegate. When Guru Dutt joined them, things became a bit awkward, especially since he was staying in another hotel, while Abrar was in the same hotel as B.R. Chopra.

But before Guru Dutt arrived and the delegation got involved with the festival, Abrar decided to utilize the time he had by making a trip to East Berlin. He remembers being very pro-Russia at the time. With Waheeda and the others accompanying him on his adventure, Abrar got the requisite permits to visit East Berlin. He remembers waiting impatiently for an hour or so at Checkpoint Charlie before he was allowed to cross the border.

Abrar describes it as a 'strange expedition' and has very clear memories of his first-ever exposure to the Russian communist ethos. The currency they had was of no use east of the Wall, and no one had warned them of this. Unable to hire taxis, the group walked all over the town, covering every bit of it on foot.

I paid dearly for I had worn new Italian shoes that day. I got the most painful corns thanks to them! The town's architecture, I noticed, was uniformly bland—rows of high-rise apartments, each with a manicured lawn in front, and some flowers at the edge of the garden. But the place lacked a soul. I also noticed that unlike to the west of the Wall, women in East Berlin hardly wore lipstick or dressed up. I concluded that the Easterners were either subjected to or preferred to observe a more spartan way of life. It was strange that the same Western psyche could be so broken into distinctly opposite mindsets and ways of life.

The screening of *Sahib Bibi Aur Ghulam* had been scheduled for 26 June. Guru Dutt landed in Berlin on 24 June as planned. When he found there was no one from his team to welcome or receive him, he was somewhat upset. He accosted Abrar when they met at the hotel. 'How come you were not there at the airport?' he asked. Abrar was quick to retort that he thought he had been sent to the Berlin Film Festival as a delegate. 'Had you told me I was here to escort you, I would definitely have been there to receive you at the airport,' he answered. Guru Dutt simply smiled at the reply, and that ended the matter. 'That was the way he was,' says Abrar.

Eventually, the screening of *Sahib Bibi Aur Ghulam* turned out to be a debacle. This despite the fact that the film had been trimmed for the festival, though at the last minute Guru Dutt put back two songs he had dropped while trimming. The film failed to make any impact. Abrar feels there were primarily two reasons for the failure.

∾

There was no emotional involvement in the theme for the Western audience. They could not empathize with the story or plight of a wife taking to drink to win her husband's love. It was a society that held no taboos against alcohol.

Also, 26 June 1963 was the day the US President, John F. Kennedy, was to visit Berlin. There was much excitement over the fact; tensions had been high throughout thanks to the Cold War that prevailed at that time. Security was tight. Kennedy was to come in the afternoon and fly off early evening. He finally landed in the city by two-thirty p.m., half an hour before the screening of *Sahib Bibi Aur Ghulam* was to begin.

I went to the theatre and looked around. It seemed that everyone was on the streets waiting to see Kennedy. There were hardly twenty-five people in the cinema hall. I told myself, why am I sitting here, in an empty hall, watching a film I have made? I left the hall and along with Waheeda and the others gathered on the terrace of the hotel, and stood on chairs, to catch a glimpse of the US President as he drove past in the motorcade.

It was quite awesome. He drove by, sitting in an open car, waving to the crowd on either side of the road. The people went wild. I learnt later that he always used the same car, it was his favourite, and so it was airlifted from city to city wherever he travelled. It was the same car I saw years later in a news documentary on his assassination.

Waheeda left Berlin for London the next day. Guru Dutt was due to start his dental treatment, and I had no reason to sit around waiting. I also took off on a mission to London. I was hesitant about making the trip, since I had no money, but B.R. Chopra insisted I accompany him. He was kind enough to say, 'Take some from me, we will square the accounts when we return to India.' I had a personal reason for wanting to go to London.

Many years ago, my brother had moved to London, and lived and worked there. I had met him when I had been to London with Guru Dutt in 1958. He was then doing a course in plastics and petroleum technology. But over the years we had heard nothing from him. Naturally, my father had been worried and had asked me to hop across from Berlin to London and check him out.

I did not find my brother in London. There had been no reply to my letters informing of my impending visit, so I went to the address in Hounslow Gardens and, as I half expected, he was not there. I went to the Pakistani and Indian High Commissions for news of him, but they could not help me find him.

Later, I discovered that he had moved to Holland and become an expert in disc brakes in Europe. I do not know why he chose to break contact with the family. Later, when General Motors realized that they were falling behind Europe in technology, they sent a team to Holland to seek out expert trainers and whisked my brother away to share his expertise and train the staff of General Motors in the US.

❦

The one notable absence from the *Sahib Bibi Aur Ghulam* team at the Berlin Film Festival was Meena Kumari. Despite her intense desire to be part of the team, she did not go. Meena Kumari often asked Abrar to talk to Kamal about letting her go to Berlin. Abrar knew that the only way Meena Kumari would be able to do so was if Kamal accompanied her. Even at the time of the National Awards function, he had told Kamal that he had to come wherever Meena Kumari went with *Sahib Bibi Aur Ghulam*. But for certain reasons Kamal could not go to Berlin as part of the delegation. And he would not let her out of his sight, and definitely not for a trip out of the country.

❦

One evening, Guru Dutt, K. Asif and I were sitting together. Asif was a bit crude in his approach to women. He thought it was manly to discuss women. He asked me, 'Have you had a silsila with Meena or not? You know she has a soft spot for writers. Her husband is a writer too.'

Guru Dutt, as was his style, did not participate in the conversation. He only smiled. Asif kept needling me. 'I cannot believe nothing happened.' I replied, 'I have brains that have been gifted to me from above, and I know that anyone who gets emotionally involved with a star faces ruin. A prime example is Kedar Sharma, so talented but his obsession with Geeta Bali made him centre every climax around his heroine, whether the story demanded it or not, and you know what that resulted in.' In fact, I added, 'My reputation of being a man obsessed with my work kept me in the clear even with Kamal himself, who did not once look at me with suspicion where his wife was concerned. That in itself is my testimony.'

❧

Though Abrar was clear of the danger of being an object of Kamal Amrohi's suspicion, it did not quite absolve Meena Kumari herself of being suspected. Abrar recounts how Kamal would have his spy and right-hand man, Baker, present even in the make-up room while Meena's make-up was being done. Abrar remembers one awful evening when, working beyond schedule to complete a shot, he had to face his heroine dissolving in tears.

❧

'Today I will get a thrashing because I am so late,' she said to me, tears streaming down her face. It was well known that not only Kamal Amrohi but even Baker would beat her quite mercilessly. Kamal exploited her monetarily too, and at one point, when she came to stay with her brother-in-law, Mehmood, the actress who had ruled Hindi cinema successfully for so many years and had been the darling of millions did not even have suitable clothes to wear.

It is another well-known fact that one of India's biggest stars died in absolute penury, having been successfully looted by her husband and by her own relatives. She lived next door to our bungalow. Her sister and nephew moved in with her and looted her methodically. There would be days when she would drop in to ask my wife for food, as there would be nothing for her to eat at her home. She would eat the leftovers or content herself with bread dipped in tea. It was tragic to see her that way. She was steadily ruining herself with drink, turning into an alcoholic, and to me it appeared as if the story of Chhoti Bahu was being repeated in real life.

22

Kaisa Pyaar Kaisi Preet Re

There has been much conjecture about the relationship between Guru Dutt and his discovery Waheeda Rehman. Parallels have been found in life as well as in cinema that seem to reflect the passion and despair that marked the relationship. Common belief has it that the sensitive director fell victim to his heroine's charms in the process of playing Pygmalion; that a chance discovery of a talented actress with a beautiful face was the beginning of the end of his emotional balance and ultimately led him to take his own life. At least three of his suicide attempts have at some point been attributed to the fact that Waheeda had over a period of time outgrown her feelings for her mentor and moved on to other banners, leaving Guru Dutt heartbroken and in a mood to end his life.

Though Abrar Alvi has the insider's view of many of the episodes surrounding the dramatis personae, and shares it for the first time ever, he is categorical that much of what has previously been said about the relationship is assessment and guesswork based on circumstantial evidence. 'Guru Dutt was too much of a gentleman to kiss and tell,' is what Abrar says. 'He never openly confessed his involvement with Waheeda to me, which means he never spoke of it to anyone else either.' But, obviously, Abrar does have first-hand knowledge of the interaction between Guru Dutt and Waheeda Rehman, and is a veritable treasure trove of information.

Despite the final tragedy and heartbreak, Abrar's memories of those days bring to life the spirit of fun and camaraderie that existed in the group. As Waheeda overcame her initial reserve and gained admission to the inner circle, she was often party to the fun and games that went on among members of the Guru Dutt Films unit. Abrar recounts many incidents that testify to the understanding that existed between the director and the actress and reveal that as they worked together in the films that unfurled under the Guru Dutt Films banner there was a subtext that ran through their relationship: Guru Dutt, the man of the world, playing mentor and guide to the simple small-town girl who was now his co-star. For example, taking his role quite seriously, Guru Dutt decided during the shooting of *Pyaasa* that Waheeda should accompany him to a nightclub.

It was all very casual. We were just sitting around in our hotel room in Calcutta, talking about this and that when the conversation veered to cabarets. Waheeda looked bewildered and asked, 'What is a cabaret?' Guru Dutt was taken aback. 'Have you never seen a cabaret?' he asked her. Waheeda and her mother, who was also in the room, shook their heads solemnly. 'That's settled then,' he said, rising with great enthusiasm. 'I will take both of you to one.'

Of course, once he had decided on something, it had to be done immediately; plans were drawn up for the same evening. Murthy was as curious as the two women; he wanted to go along too, as did some of the other members of the unit who were present. But Guru Dutt had other plans. He was not going to let a gaggle of men spoil his little adventure. He looked at Murthy for a long moment, then moved into the inner room, motioning me to follow.

He opened his cupboard where his clothes were neatly hung and offered me a jacket. 'Try this one for size, see if it fits you,' he said. I obeyed without question. There was always a reason for his actions. The jacket fit me just fine. 'That's settled then,' he said, and went back to the room where the others were.

The two women had left to change. Murthy sat there waiting to know what we proposed to do. 'Do you have a jacket?' Guru Dutt asked his cinematographer. Needless to say, Murthy did not have one, and even if he did, had not brought it along on location.

'Too bad,' Guru Dutt said. 'We'll have to go without you. A jacket is a must at the clubs that feature cabarets.' Turning to me, he said, 'Luckily you have one, Abrar, you may come along!'

Another time, we—Guru Dutt, his assistant Niranjan, Ram Singh and I—were sitting at the studio, chatting, when I was told that someone wanted to see me urgently. I was not in a mood to be disturbed and did not want to break up our conversation, so I said, 'Please ask the person to wait,' and turned back to the group.

A few minutes later, the reminder came: it was a woman and she wanted to see me. Guru Dutt began to rag me. 'Who is this secret admirer?' he quizzed. 'You are a *chhupa rustam*.'

I was embarrassed and waved away his words, but he grew serious and said, 'You must not keep a woman waiting. Go and talk to her, find out what it's about. We are all here anyway—you can always come back and join us.'

I left them and went across to the waiting room. There was a woman in a burkha. I requested her to sit down and asked her what she wanted. She told me she had come from far to meet me. She had seen all of Guru Dutt's films and admired me immensely as a writer. I was of course flattered, but still perplexed, and asked her what she wanted of me. She wished to act in films, she said, and wanted my advice on the choice of roles and an introduction to Guru Dutt. I told her that I could not gauge her looks or her age or even her histrionic abilities if she chose to hide behind a black curtain, and that she would have to take off her naqab and reveal her face if she wanted me to help in any way.

She was adamant, she could not, would not take off her burkha, but she kept asking me to help her, entreating me. She was sounding quite desperate. At some point, I began to realize that there was something familiar about her. I decided to call her bluff. 'If you don't show me your face, I shall be forced to take off the covering from it,' I said loudly and made as if to move towards her. Suddenly, she burst into a loud peal of laughter, which was echoed by the group that stood concealed behind the door.

Guru Dutt had set the scene up, and Waheeda, enjoying herself thoroughly, proved that she could indeed play a part very well!

Abrar is sure that in the beginning at least the romantic in Guru Dutt saw in Waheeda the perfect foil to his creative and intellectual leanings. A deeper 'relationship', however, developed not because she played Galatea to his Pygmalion, but because Guru Dutt himself had a troubled and tumultuous married life. His relationship with wife Geeta was, at most times, cause for much personal angst.

For one, she was already an established singer and star by the time he married her, while he was still finding his feet as a director and seeking his place in the filmi firmament. And, unlike her husband, Geeta was an extrovert with a wide circle of Bengali friends, among whom were singer–music director Hemant Kumar and his wife; Manna Ladda, the distributor from Bengal; Biren Nag, the art director of *Sahib Bibi Aur Ghulam* who later made *Bees Saal Baad*; Hemen Gupta of *Anandmath* fame and his wife; and Smriti

Biswas, Geeta's closest friend. Abrar narrates one particular incident that throws light on the complex relationship between Guru Dutt and his wife's friends' circle.

∾

For whatever reason, Guru Dutt did not like hobnobbing with this group, and liked Smriti Biswas the least; he always thought she was a bad influence on his wife. Niranjan and I had been dispatched to the annexe of Guru Dutt's house to flesh out the screenplay of *Pyaasa*. Guru Dutt would often drop in with a casual, 'How far has it gone?' to check how the work was progressing.

One day we had settled down to discuss the progression of the screenplay. It was evening, and we could hear a few cars drawing up. Looking out we saw a blue convertible and a green one standing outside, and before we could react, the entire group—Hemant Kumar and his wife, Mr and Mrs Manna Ladda, Mr and Mrs Hemen Gupta, among others—walked in. They were boisterous, demanding liquor, obviously in a mood to party.

We had been trying to work out a scene, and Guru Dutt was resentful of the invasion and resultant interruption, but he smiled to hide his irritation, and decided to play host. Soon, a card game was under way, glasses were being filled and the liquor started flowing. They invited me to play, but I turned them down politely, saying, 'I can't afford to play flush with you big shots at my salary,' and they let me be.

At some point in the evening, the liquor ran out. One male member of the group got up, smoothed his clothes and said, 'I will go and get some.' Almost immediately, one of the women got up saying, 'I need something too, I will go with you.' When the two did not return for what seemed to me a considerable time, I asked Guru Dutt, 'When will they be back?'

For the first time I saw Guru Dutt being indiscreet. He said to me, 'They have gone together, you should understand why.'

I was flummoxed for a moment before everything fell into place. I realized why Guru Dutt was averse to the group that his wife belonged to: he was aware of their penchant to share partners. I don't know if Geeta and he fought over this group and its influence on her, but this was the only time he mentioned his open dislike of them to me, and that too in an indirect way.

Abrar worked closely with Waheeda while grooming her for *CID* and *Pyaasa*. In the process he grew quite close to her mother, who saw in him someone solid and dependable, someone who could be an elder brother to her daughter. Waheeda also endeared herself to almost everyone who came in contact with her. She was unfailingly polite, soft-spoken, and yet possessed a lot of determination, a burning desire to learn and succeed. Abrar wonders where the Guru Dutt–Waheeda Rehman relationship would have gone, if fate had played a different card.

In some way, we fanned the flames. Many of us in the unit felt that Waheeda was infinitely more suitable as a partner for Guru Dutt than his wife Geeta. Guru Dutt's mother too shared our opinion. In fact, she was a huge influence on him and he was in awe of her. In fact, digressing from the subject, I must mention that one of the reasons he took me on was because his mother approved of me. She was in a way my first examiner at Guru Dutt Films. She questioned me in great detail and recommended me to Guru Dutt because of my skills with conversational dialogue. So her encouragement, albeit subtle, on the matter of Waheeda must have swayed him considerably. And I think we made this obvious to them without even knowing we did so. He would pack up shooting at any time without provocation, and make any excuse to be alone with her, even sending me away. Often he would say to me, 'I do not know why I cannot overwhelm her . . .' And that from as private a man as he, was as good as a declaration of involvement.

I think it was during the premiere of *CID*, in Calcutta, that people first started getting an inkling of the budding relationship. Guru Dutt, Waheeda, her mother and other members of the unit of *CID* had gone to attend the premiere, along with Johnny Walker and music director Ravi. By then, Guru Dutt was in the habit of taking sleeping tablets at night. I did not go, but I heard of the developments there.

For one, Ravi got Guru Dutt to swear to kick off the sleeping tablet habit. The catalyst for this was the fact that at the function, when it was the producer's turn to speak, Guru Dutt was garbled and incoherent. He could not articulate his thoughts properly, was slurring his words. Such a dismal performance in public embarrassed not just his friends but the director himself.

The second development seemed to be the growing attraction Waheeda felt towards her co-star and director. Waheeda's mother would ask me often, on their return, 'Abrar, what will happen to my daughter? I worry about her.' Her fears were well founded. 'My daughter is not the type to flit from man to man, and he is a married man,' she would say to me. 'She tells me that he says he will give up his life for her.' She knew I was close to Guru Dutt and probably hoped I would ask him of his intentions.

Guru Dutt's unhappiness with the state of his conjugal life was clear to me from the *Pyaasa* days. In fact, his first attempt at suicide was during *Pyaasa*. It might have been the result of a particularly bad skirmish with Geeta or because he was at an emotional low. He might have found Waheeda a source of comfort; love on the rebound is a common enough occurrence, and he had reason to feel that his married life had little meaning for either Geeta or himself.

Personally, I still do not understand what could have prompted Guru Dutt to pursue his attraction for Waheeda. My assessment is that he was a romantic who could have continued in the role of thwarted husband and silent lover, but fed up with the stalemate of his conjugal life, he may well have felt drawn to her.

One day he came bursting in, radiant, and looking me full in the eye, said in a man-to-man tone, 'You know, Abrar, there is nothing wrong with me.' Even today I do not know exactly what he meant, but I think he meant he had at last been able to get as close to Waheeda as he had hoped to get. Yet, I have reason to believe that the relationship, though intensely passionate, was purely emotional and platonic.

Abrar is categorical that Geeta was in some ways to blame for the growing closeness between Guru Dutt and Waheeda. Her immature behaviour and suspicious nature made Guru Dutt seek solace in Waheeda. He narrates two incidents which throw light on this aspect of Geeta's mental make-up. The first took place at the time the writer and the director were preparing to go to London before the shooting of *Kagaaz Ke Phool*. Guru Dutt was embarking on his search for a lens that could shoot in cinemascope and convert to 35mm, and he had wanted Abrar to go along.

Geeta had by then realized that Guru Dutt was close to me, and that I had an influence on him. That is probably why one morning she came over to my house. My wife came to tell me, 'Geeta has come.'

I thought it was Geeta Bali, but she said, 'No, it is Mrs Dutt.'

I met her, and she put on what I now believe was a great act, even shedding a few tears. I think, seeing that the mother of my children was also present, she thought she could enlist her help, woman to woman, to work on me, to influence her husband.

'Please understand me,' she said, 'I am at my wits' end, helpless. You are travelling with him, please try to reason with him, he is crazy about Waheeda.'

I told her, 'I know Waheeda very well by now. There is nothing between them. Please understand that if he does anything that breaks the sanctity of married life, there are at least two people in his unit, Niranjan and me, who will not work with him after that. He has become a father, and we will not brook any irresponsibility on his part towards his children.'

She listened quietly and left. But before she went, she dried her eyes, and said in a very calm voice, 'Don't tell him I was here.'

I believe she came only to verify her suspicions. And though I gave Guru Dutt a clean chit, it did little to allay Geeta's doubts. She was influenced a lot by Smriti Biswas, who also taught her ways to test whether her suspicions were valid and, if possible, catch her husband red-handed.

One day, Guru Dutt handed me a letter. 'Read it,' he said. I opened it gingerly and saw that it was signed 'Yours, Waheeda'. I looked at him, but he said again, 'Read it.'

The letter was a torrid declaration of love. It said: 'I need to talk to you, I can't hold myself back, so I am writing to you, you have driven me to distraction, I am losing my senses, I don't know what you have done to me . . .' And so on. The letter ended with a request for an assignation. 'Today at 6.30 to 7, meet me at Nariman Point.'

When I looked up after reading the letter, Guru Dutt asked, 'What do you think?'

I replied, 'I don't think Waheeda has written this.'

'I agree,' Guru Dutt said.

I said, 'You meet her every day, have enough opportunity to meet her in private, in her make-up room. Why would she write this, and why would she want to meet you in a public place like Nariman Point? Why call you there?'

We decided on a plan. He would drive towards Nariman Point and stop near the Cricket Club of India. I would, in my car, take another road, and check out who came there.

I took my second-hand khatara car and parked it in the by-lane next to the CCI. I knew where Guru Dutt was waiting and watching. I saw a car approach and slow down near Nariman Point. Geeta Dutt and Smriti Biswas were sitting in the backseat of the chauffeur-driven car. It moved to the Nariman Point area, waited and watched and then moved on to Marine Drive. I followed the car and went back to Guru Dutt who had seen the whole drama.

I think this was the first time, that night after going home, that he confronted Geeta with the episode and, as he confessed to me later, raised his hand on her.

A strange incident happened during the shooting of *Sahib Bibi Aur Ghulam*. It throws some light on the state of affairs in Guru Dutt's personal life at that time. Waheeda was sure of her status as a practising Muslim. She was also sure that she would marry only a Muslim. According to Abrar, it was because of Rauf—husband of Waheeda's sister Sayeeda—that things went out of hand.

Rauf, we discovered as we got to know him better, was a crook. He managed in the long run to exploit both his wife and her family. He went to town with the information that Waheeda had told Sayeeda that Guru Dutt was willing to convert to Islam. He, in fact, went to the extent of announcing it at the Jama Masjid in Bombay. It was a Friday, and at namaz time there was quite a gathering of the devout there. Taking the opportunity, Rauf declared publicly, 'Listen my friends, there's good news. The famous director Guru Dutt is going to become a Muslim and marry my sister-in-law, Waheeda.'

I knew nothing of this. When his driver suddenly turned up and demanded I go with him because I was wanted at Guru Dutt's house, I got into the car and went along. I was used to such summons—it could be to discuss a new storyline or because Guru Dutt wanted to share with me his wonder at watching a chicken hatch.

On reaching his house, I saw M. Sadiq, the director of *Chaudhvin Ka Chand*, Rehman and Johnny Walker. It struck me that all of them were Muslims, but I still had no clue why they were there. Guru Dutt was not around. I asked where he was, what had happened. Why had I been sent for?

They told me, 'He is at the back. Rauf has made a public statement at the Jama Masjid that Guru wants to marry Waheeda and is willing to convert. Rauf is coming to take Guru Dutt to the nikkah ceremony. A qazi is coming along, and so are witnesses, and it's going to be a big mess.'

Guru Dutt was understandably in a panic. He was reserved about his emotions and his personal life, and this was not just embarrassing but had put him in a tight spot for no fault of his.

I said, 'Let Rauf come. We'll see.' I had handled Rauf before, and knew just how to deal with him. I would call his bluff. Rauf drove up in a Fiat with a friend. He stomped up to us and said, 'Get him now, I need to speak with him.'

An altercation ensued. But, once he realized he was beaten and had no leg to stand on, Rauf went away. Matters could have turned very ugly, but the situation was saved. I do not know if and how Waheeda heard of the incident and how both her brother-in-law's behaviour and Guru Dutt's affected her.

∾

Interestingly enough, in an oblique way, Geeta Dutt was responsible for the eventual break-up between her husband and Waheeda. When the fracas about Rauf and Guru Dutt's alleged intention of converting to Islam happened, Geeta was in London. It was fortunate for Guru Dutt that he was spared the embarrassment of having his wife witness or hear about the entire mess. But another shock awaited him.

∾

Geeta did not come home from London. She went to Kashmir instead. When days passed into weeks and she showed no inclination to come to Bombay, Guru Dutt began to press upon her to return. At which point, Geeta sent a message that she had fallen from a horse and broken a collarbone. She could not travel for the next few weeks. Ever the concerned husband, Guru Dutt, unable to leave for Kashmir himself, sent his assistant, Shyam Kapoor, to help Geeta through the rough patch. Shyam came back sooner than expected with quite a different story.

He had discovered that there was nothing wrong with Geeta; her collarbone was quite intact, and the real reason for her continued absence was a rather personable young man who was seen in her company. The personable young man, it was discovered, was a Pakistani settled in London, who had a British passport and who had followed Geeta to Kashmir. It was news too bitter for Guru Dutt to swallow.

At the bottom of it all, he was quite the chauvinist. He could not face the fact that he was being cuckolded and knew it too. He also believed that a man could sow his wild oats, have his bit of fun, but women were not supposed to be anything but constant and faithful to their husbands.

Even when I planned to marry a woman who was not well read and belonged to a different station in life from me or him, he remonstrated with me saying, 'You do not have to marry her, you will ruin your life if you do so . . . all these things have to be finished with a "jhatka".' And he had made the sign of a slaughter. Now, faced with the possibility that Geeta could be seeing another man, he took quick steps to ensure his wife remained his, by right.

I did not know of Guru Dutt's decision till it had already been implemented. This was during the final days of the shooting of *Sahib Bibi Aur Ghulam*. One day, Waheeda came to me and burst out, 'What's wrong with him? What has happened to him? I don't understand.' It was only then that I discovered that Guru Dutt had spurned the very woman he had wooed so arduously and 'overwhelmed' with his love so recently.

Waheeda had, till then, free access to the make-up rooms in the Guru Dutt Films set-up. She would come to the studio to get her make-up done even when she was shooting for other films. Her make-up room was adjoining Guru Dutt's, and right in front, guarding both the inner rooms, was Guruswamy's room.

One day, as she was walking to her make-up room, Guru Dutt's Man Friday, Ratan, blocked her way. He would not allow her to enter the room, and she was forced to turn back. There was no explanation. The next day, the same thing happened again. That was when she burst into my room, almost in tears. I realized then that to get Geeta back into his life, Guru Dutt had dropped Waheeda like a hot brick. He made the sacrifice to assuage his hurt male ego.

I accosted him and told him, 'I never encouraged you to have an affair, but what you are doing now is wrong. I believe, as you do, that no man who is a father should look at women other than his wife, but of course such things happen all the time. In your case I might even justify it at some level, because you were not happy in your marriage; you had made the wrong choice. When you pursued her, overwhelmed her with your attentions, we kept quiet, because your sister, your mother, Sayeeda and even I felt she was more suited for you. You cannot drop her without some real reason.'

But Guru Dutt would not discuss the matter with me. It was as if he had suddenly built a wall between me and the subject. He just would not listen to anything I had to say about Waheeda. I never found out why, as he never explained his reasons to me. The fact remains that Waheeda soon stopped coming to the studio. Anyway, we had finished shooting her part in the film, and there was no reason for her to visit the studio, other than to meet Guru Dutt.

Guru Dutt repaired his relationship with Geeta. He found a certain measure of conjugal happiness again, and the two took off to Srinagar for a second honeymoon. But Abrar, the director, had a new problem. The last scene of *Sahib Bibi Aur Ghulam* required Waheeda's presence. Waheeda, of course, was not around. And Guru Dutt would not ask her either. In fact, he asked Abrar if they could avoid having her in the scene. But Abrar told him her presence was essential. It was left to Abrar to approach his heroine and request her to complete the film.

Waheeda was shooting at that time in what is now Natraj Studio, and when I spoke to her about the last scene which required her presence, she said quietly and with firm determination, 'I will not step inside that studio.'

I said, 'You have always said I am like the elder brother you never had. I am requesting you now to respect my wish. I am making a film for the first time, and you must help me make it well.'

It took a lot of persuasion to get her to agree, and even then, she came up with all of thirty-six conditions. 'I'll come,' she finally said, 'but I will not let him touch me, I will not talk, or have any dialogues.'

I said, 'I have worked out the scene, you won't have to talk to him, you will touch him, that's all.'

She wanted to know why I was insisting on her touching Guru Dutt. It took a lot of explaining. I told her that in the scene she had to comfort a man who is upset at the crumbling of a past; the haveli he had once loved was being broken down under his supervision, he was having to get on with the job though it tore at his heart. 'There are no dialogues, it's all in close-up,' I said and finally Waheeda agreed.

❧

On the appointed day, the actress who had been the ruling star in all his films since he discovered her, came to the set, and without a word or glance at Guru Dutt, gave her shot and left. She was to meet him only once more during his lifetime, two years later, in 1963, when Waheeda accompanied Abrar to the Berlin Film Festival in which *Sahib Bibi Aur Ghulam* was the official Indian entry.

They hardly exchanged a word during the time they were in Berlin, and soon after the screening, she went to London. It was Abrar who helped her by giving her a contact—an influential businessman friend, Gaurisaria, also known as the 'jute king'—she could turn to in case she needed help in that city. Abrar wrote to Gaurisaria asking him to help Waheeda in case she should fall short of foreign exchange and require some money.

❧

I got rapped for that letter. Gaurisaria's loyalties lay with Guru Dutt, and he told him about my letter. Guru Dutt reprimanded me, saying, 'Is this why I introduced you to Gaurisaria? So that you can ask him to lend money to anybody at all?' It was most unlike him to make a statement like that, but I did not mind the reprimand. However, the fact that he had so successfully killed the relationship saddened me.

23

Ghar Ki Barbadi Ke
Asaar Nazar Aate Hain

Despite Abrar Alvi's refusal to write or direct the remake of *President*, Guru Dutt decided to go ahead with the remake, which he titled *Baharen Phir Bhi Aayengi*. He chose Shahid Lateef as its director. Lateef had made *Sone Ki Chidiya* way back in 1958 and in the wake of its success, waiting for something bigger to come his way, had refused many offers. The long wait had proved in vain and depleted his resources. Guru Dutt decided that getting Lateef to direct *Baharen* would not only put his skills to good use, but also rescue the man out of his despondency and the hard times he had fallen into. Lateef's wife, the celebrated Urdu writer Ismat Chughtai, was given the task of writing the screenplay. Binoy Chatterjee, who had written the 1937 version of *President*, was also called in to guide the writing of the screenplay.

But even as the film went on the floors, and Lateef had shot just about four reels, the keen critic in Guru Dutt realized that there was not enough in what had been shot to satisfy his high standards. He wasted no time in calling his friend and trusted aide.

'I am scrapping what has been shot,' he told me. 'You write it, I'll direct it.' I had no choice but to comply, I just could not ignore the emotional and intellectual bond. But there was the matter of Lateef. Guru Dutt assigned the ever-willing Guruswamy the unpleasant task of giving Lateef his marching orders, but Lateef had influential friends. He appealed to K. Asif, who was at that time directing Guru Dutt in *Love and God*. And Asif requested his hero to let Lateef remain on the sets.

Guru Dutt demurred. 'People will know he is a dummy, they know I am directing the film,' he argued.

'The world knows he has been signed on to direct the film. If you throw him out now, the disgrace will kill him,' Asif implored, and Guru Dutt agreed to let Lateef stay on the sets. His job was to say 'Action' and 'Cut' in the scenes where Guru Dutt faced the camera.

Guru Dutt's fondness for Bengal influenced his latest film too. He infused the film with shades of Bengal. The hero lives with his mother, and his sister—played by Geeta Dutt's sister—who lives with them wears Bengali saris. He shot a scene where the hero goes fishing, and that too was set against a typically Bengal backdrop. It wasn't at all essential for the film to be set in Bengal, but, as Abrar says, Guru Dutt wouldn't have it any other way.

'There was really no reason to take the unit to Bengal. He could have shot the film anywhere, but no, only Bengal would do,' Abrar says. So off they went to shoot a sequence at the Martin Burn railway which existed at the time only in Bengal. It was a narrow gauge track and the train could be overtaken by walkers, and Guru Dutt wanted Abrar to create a sequence around this.

When work started on the new script and screenplay for

Baharen, Abrar ran headlong into conflict with Binoy Chatterjee. It did not take much time for Guru Dutt to realize that Abrar and he would be handling his new film together, with no one else in between. 'I have the habit of analysing everything that is set before me, and being extremely logical and critical,' Abrar explains. 'Before long I took apart the screenplay that Binoy Chatterjee had put together.'

Through the shooting of *Baharen*, Guru Dutt also continued to shoot a lot in the south for other banners. Abrar would often accompany him. He narrates a funny incident that took place during one of these trips, in what would turn out to be one of their last journeys together.

∾

We were all in Madras, shooting for a south production. There was Guru Dutt, music director Ravi and I. We would finish the day's work and sit in Guru Dutt's room, drinking and swapping tales and having dinner.

One day, Ravi picked up the phone and told the manager, 'Send a plate of Chicken a la Kiev to my room tonight.' I wondered why he needed more food that night, but realizing that he might be a man of appetite, said nothing. Ravi asked me if we would like a plate each too. I demurred, but Guru Dutt said, why not. He was always ready for anything new, and a plate of extra food, he said, would not hurt in any way. A plate each was ordered for both of us.

The matter rested there and the evening went on. When we finally decided to turn in, we bid goodnight, made plans for the next morning, and went to our respective rooms.

To my utter surprise, when I got into bed, a bit hazy with the food and drink and the tiredness of a long day, there was a woman cuddled under the sheets. I jumped out of bed, thinking I had got into the wrong room, but soon discovered that she was the Chicken a la Kiev we had so unwittingly ordered.

～

Abrar is tight-lipped on what his friend and director did with the chicken in his room, but insists that he sent his dish back untasted.

Baharen was to cause Guru Dutt much grief. By the time he had shot about twelve reels, the director had lost faith in his subject. 'Somehow he knew that the film would not succeed,' Abrar says. He lost all enthusiasm and would gladly have scrapped it as was his way with things he did not find up to the mark, but he was too far gone, too committed to back out. He had taken a loan to make the film and there was no going back.

'I really don't know whether the turmoil over his latest project contributed to his suicide,' Abrar says. The fact was that, unlike in the past, when Guru Dutt closed a project summarily the moment he decided that he was unhappy with the way it was turning out, with no thought of the money spent, the director was forced to keep going with *Baharen*, even though his heart was not in it. In fact, Abrar and he were working on the script even on that fateful night when Guru Dutt decided to take his own life.

There was no premonition, absolutely no warning. If there had been any inkling, Abrar says, he would have hung around and kept his friend and mentor company; he would have ensured that the loneliness, the depression, did not overcome Guru Dutt, leading him to the point of no return.

The evening was like any other with Guru Dutt pondering over his project, though in the throes of a dark mood, while Abrar toiled on the next set of scenes. Perhaps it was coincidental that the scene Abrar was working on was the one in which the heroine dies a sad, lonely death. Thwarted in love, with her loved one being the lover of her younger sister, the broken-hearted woman has nothing to live for, and it is the depression that causes her death.

It was a delicate scene to write and one that needed concentration and a fine balance, if it was not to slip into the maudlin. Abrar worried the scene like a dog worries a bone, looking at it in his typical fashion, logically and critically. Guru Dutt would infuse the sequence with emotion while shooting it. Abrar's role was to ensure that it made practical sense and kept the story credible and logical.

The evening rolled on, with a friend dropping in, bouts of drinking and desultory talk. Guru Dutt was not in the mood for chatter, and Abrar was too engrossed with the job on hand. There was a series of phone calls to and from Geeta Dutt. Abrar did not know then what had transpired between Guru Dutt and his estranged wife during those calls—the phone was downstairs.

As the night dragged on, the visitor was persuaded to have his dinner by himself, and having to go to work the next day, took his leave. Guru Dutt was by then in a foul mood. His conversations with Geeta had made him bitter and melancholic. Even after all these years that evening plays in Abrar's mind like an unending roll of film in a projector.

As it was, he had been drinking since early evening—his Man Friday had mentioned that to me—and it had left him with a strangely sullen disposition. I tried to get him out of it, but not only did I fail, I also had to watch helplessly as he sank deeper into melancholy.

Worse still, he refused to have his dinner with the visitor and insisted on waiting for me, drinking steadily. He was really embittered and mentioned a tiff with Geeta over their two-and-a-half-year-old daughter visiting him. He wanted her to come over and Geeta was adamant that she would not send the child. Guru Dutt had told her the refusal would cost her his life or something to that effect.

I wish I had sensed that those words were more seriously meant than I had thought at that time. I was not sharing his quarters as I had done often in the past. I was on contract with Lekh, on his new film, and when I was done with my writing for Guru Dutt, I planned to leave for Lekh's house to retire for the night, as there was a morning schedule.

By the time I finished my scene, it was almost midnight. Guru Dutt agreed to sit for dinner, but ate nothing. I was hungry. I polished off a meal to my complete satisfaction. Guru Dutt was not quite drunk, he could hold his liquor well, but his mood was decidedly terrible. I wanted to read the script to him, but he was in no frame of mind to listen to it. That should have been a warning.

~

Guru Dutt told Abrar to leave the script with Ratan. 'If you don't mind I would like to retire,' he said, and got up to go to his room. These would be the last words Abrar would hear from the man with whom he had shared the ten most creative years of his life.

There is nothing to prove that his unhappiness with the way his latest film was shaping up was one of the causes behind his suicide, but the fact remains, sadly and irrevocably, that before he could complete his film, Guru Dutt was dead. The story of one of India's most sensitive film-makers had prematurely come to an end.

Epilogue

The grief over his mentor's death was overwhelming, but Abrar had little time to indulge in mourning. Not only was *Baharen* lying incomplete, Abrar was also aware that Guru Dutt had taken a loan to make the film. Handling the creditors was important as was trying to get the film back on track with a new cast and crew, including a new hero to replace Guru Dutt. Above all, Abrar wanted to keep Guru Dutt Films alive, as a tribute to its founder. Once work at Guru Dutt Films resumed, it was considered only logical that Guru Dutt's brother, Atma Ram, would take on the unfinished project.

A distributors' conference, led by Guru Dutt's Delhi and Calcutta distributors, took place. Though the distributors did not have any big financial stake in the film, they decided to steer its fate. They told Atma Ram that though he was the legal and natural heir to Guru Dutt's legacy, Abrar, by virtue of having worked with Guru Dutt closely, was his creative successor.

In short, the distributors made it clear to Atma Ram that if he wanted to direct the film, they were not interested; they would rather let their investment sink. If Atma wanted them to take up the film and distribute it, it would have to be handed over to Abrar Alvi to direct. Engrossed as he was with other practical difficulties in keeping Guru Dutt Films running, Abrar was unaware of these developments.

∽

I knew nothing of this meeting till a delegation led by K.G. Prabhakar, who was Murthy's assistant and the film's cameraman, the film's editor, Y.G. Chavan, and the dress and make-up man, Baburao, came to me. 'You have to take up the film,' they pleaded, 'otherwise Guru Dutt Films will close.'

I was literally left holding the baby. The project I had refused was thrust upon me. I had to take it on to keep the flag of Guru Dutt Films flying. *Baharen Phir Bhi Aayengi* had to be completed. It was Atma's golden chance to finally direct a film and he had announced that he would take up the megaphone to complete the film. Everyone knew that Shahid Lateef was director only in name and was a dummy for Guru Dutt. But the distributors remained adamant on not wanting Atma as director.

I had no choice. I definitely wanted the banner's name to continue and so I started to save the equipment that would otherwise have been sold cheaply to pay back the ten lakh rupees that Guru Dutt had taken on loan.

Abrar sealed his commitment to the venture by returning the advance monies that others had given him to write their films. *Teesri Kasam* for Shailendra was one of them. His own pet project based on Premchand's 'Kafan', written for the screen as *Nai Chunariyan*, which he wanted to direct, was definitely the most heart-rending of his sacrifices. Producer F.C. Mehra had already announced in the booklet that he had brought out to publicize *Professor*: 'Await our next film, *Nai Chunariyan*, written and directed by Abrar Alvi.'

Guru Dutt had rejected 'Kafan' outright when Abrar had proposed it as the project he wanted to take up after *Sahib Bibi Aur Ghulam*. Abrar found in the story a pathos and realism that would match that of the earlier film which had won for the producer and his banner so many accolades. But Guru Dutt had dismissed the idea. 'It's such a morose theme, such a loser's story!' he had announced. 'Why would anyone want to watch such a film?'

It was while he was working on *Baharen* that Guru Dutt discovered that his writer had not given up his pet project after all.

❧

When he had asked me to take on *Baharen* and work with him, I told him I had other commitments and had signed on with other banners. Later, when he was seriously thinking of canning *Baharen* and was looking for a new story, a common friend, an income tax officer, Gole, suggested a story by well-known Marathi writer P.K. Atre. He asked me to convince Guru Dutt to take it up. I listened to the story and narrated my adaptation of Premchand's 'Kafan'. Gole was very impressed.

I had committed the adaptation to F.C. Mehra of Eagle Films by then. A few days later, Guru Dutt broached the subject with me: 'Gole tells me you have a story; why not share it with me?' I told him that I had already promised it to someone else. He became sarcastic and wanted to know what stories I had 'peddled' to other banners. I remember his exact words. '*Achha bhai*,' he said, '*badey producer ke liye aap likhte hain, chhote producer hain hum . . . hamen sunaiye, ek do suggestion hi shayad de saken.*' I narrated the story over the next two and a half hours. He said, 'Good.' I said mockingly, '*Adaab arz hai*, so you have recognized its merits.' I could not resist adding, 'But *janab*, why is it you covet the story now. It is morbid, a story about losers. Don't you remember what you had said about Premchand's "Kafan"? Well, this is the same story retold by me.'

He said, 'Make it for me; you won't get the same facilities from Mehra as you get here. Do it for me. Only one condition: no stars.'

I told him that I had already signed Meena Kumari and Nutan and was waiting for their dates. He would not give up. 'You will have to compromise if you take them—they are stars. I want you to make it your way, as you see it with your third eye. I will help, give you time. Take new artists, train them for six months. Make it for me.'

I agreed. But ten days after this conversation, he was gone, leaving *Baharen* and the prospect of *Nai Chunariyan* behind.

∼

One and a half years were to pass after his mentor's death before Abrar Alvi could take up work on *Baharen Phir Bhi Aayengi* again. The first hurdle was finding a replacement for Guru Dutt. Atma Ram had tried and failed, there was no known actor quite like Guru Dutt in looks, which was a prerequisite if at least some of the reels that had been shot featuring him were to be saved.

When the choice moved from lookalikes to other known actors, Atma Ram ran into fresh trouble. Both Dev Anand and Joy Mukherji, who were approached, turned down the offer. 'Perhaps they were superstitious about taking on a film whose male lead had died midway,' Abrar says. Whatever the reason, Abrar, now left holding the reins of the production and still smarting at having to give up two dream projects, was beginning to get edgy.

Finally, he took it upon himself to find the male lead to replace Guru Dutt. He told Atma Ram, 'I will find you a hero: he is saleable, and also a bit known in the industry.' Acting rather mysterious and without divulging the name of the actor he was approaching, Abrar sent a man carrying a letter from him to an actor in Amritsar. The missive got an immediate response. Abrar and *Baharen* had their new hero: Dharmendra.

The inside story of why a rising star said yes to Abrar's request with such alacrity, particularly for a film which was being talked of as being jinxed, in an industry driven by superstition, is interesting.

Abrar had first met Dharmendra many years ago, quite by accident. *Filmfare* had set up a talent hunt, and Bimal Roy and Guru Dutt were closely involved in it as sponsors. They were also the main members of the jury. Both directors valued young, new talent and thought this was a good way to unearth it from among the thousands who dreamt of becoming film stars.

The contest evoked an amazing response, and the sponsoring directors had a tough time wading through the entries that showed promise. Finally, after much deliberation, the choice was narrowed down to six finalists. The finalists were called to Bombay, and were housed in a lodge, where they sized each other up, secretly sharpening their skills, as they waited for the final test.

Unfortunately, just before the finals, Bimal Roy fell ill, and the venue was shifted to Central Studio, where Guru Dutt had once shot certain portions of *Kaagaz Ke Phool*. Central Studio does not exist any more. Its place has been taken by the once-teeming, bustling Air Conditioned or A/C Market, which also over the years has felt the keen edge of neglect thanks to the swank new malls that have sprung up all over Bombay. But in those years, the studio was privy to large cars driving up and a bevy of famous faces alighting to rush inside to don grease paint and face the moving cameras.

All would have gone smoothly, if it had not been for a second coincidence. On the day of the test, Guru Dutt was summoned to attend a court case. Abrar, was, as was his wont, left holding the baby.

❧

Guru Dutt asked me to conduct the test. 'Check their faces, profiles, dialogue delivery,' he instructed and rushed off. As was expected, most of the boys who had turned up had hairstyles like the one Dev Anand sported. Only one of them had a crew cut, his hair was about an inch long and grew straight upwards. In most other circumstances, it would have been quite ordinary, but here it was almost dramatic in its difference. The finalists went through the tests I subjected them to and left, the crew-cut boy included. When Guru Dutt returned, he asked how the entire process had gone.

I told him it was okay, but that there was only one boy who stood out and seemed to hold promise. However, I added, the boy's dialogue delivery was insipid, there was hardly any modulation. As chief dialogue writer and modulator in most of Guru Dutt's productions, it was but natural that I noticed these aspects immediately.

'Who is he like?' Guru Dutt asked me.

'Nobody,' I said. 'He is himself, he has no pretensions, no set notions. The boy seems an original, and it might be possible to mould him, develop his personality.'

The crew cut had just the opposite effect the boy's father had hoped it would. Knowing that his son had dreams of becoming an actor, the schoolteacher father had taken the scissors to his head and trimmed off his hair. But, instead of damning him, the cut actually set him apart, marking him out as a man with a mind of his own. *Filmfare* published photographs of the new find, Dharmendra. It looked as though the boy would find a place in Guru Dutt's next film. But nothing came of Guru Dutt's interest in the new actor or his potential. It was Bimal Roy who would give Dharmendra his first big break with a small but strong role in *Bandini*.

Almost a decade later, with *Baharen* staring him in the face, Abrar decided that it was time to cash in on his goodwill with a star he had helped discover. He had met Dharmendra again, years later, in Madras. By that time, the star had done a few films, and there were also reports of a romance with Meena Kumari, who was paired opposite the dashing newcomer in what was to be his breakthrough film, *Phool Aur Patthar*. In fact, it was when Abrar dropped in to see Meena Kumari that he ran into Dharmendra.

❦

It had been a long time since *Sahib Bibi Aur Ghulam* and Meena Kumari was happy to meet me. She offered to have dinner served in her room, so we could continue talking. But I told her I would eat later, there was a 'friend' waiting in my room. Of course, they knew that I meant the bottle of liquor I normally had before dinner. I signalled to Dharmendra. 'Come on, hero,' I said, 'let's go and share a drink before we eat.' Dharmendra demurred, but I told Meena, 'He drinks, he is only playing the innocent.'

I was like an elder brother to Dharmendra. I took him to my room, and as the evening wore on, he got a bit sentimental. He spoke about the test, and how I had been very gentle with him. I said, 'You are doing well . . .' to which he told me that whenever I wanted him, for whatever kind of role, he would be ready to sign on. 'I'll come,' he said simply. I asked him how much he charged and Dharmendra replied, 'If you decide that I can do the role, if you are interested in casting me, pay me anything from one paisa to one lakh, and I will do it.'

And that is why, when we were stuck for a hero for *Baharen*'s relaunch, I decided to send a letter to Dharmendra, who was at the time shooting for the Punjabi film *Ek Chadar Maili Si* with Geeta Bali, reminding him of his promise. I wrote to him about our meeting in Madras, and his words to me, and added that the time had come for him to redeem his promise. 'If you don't do this film,' I wrote, 'the company which discovered you as a hero will die—the camera will be sold, nothing will remain.' Dharmendra read the letter and told the bearer, 'This film will be made.' He gave the dates for it almost immediately.

We started shooting for *Baharen* a few months later. Now it was my turn to make the stars of the film 'cry'. I was a hard taskmaster. I needed full concentration on the sets. Both Tanuja and Mala Sinha were used to being flippant. Tanuja would crack jokes and laugh with Dharmendra; one reproach from me and Dharam would obey, but Tanuja was incorrigible. She was like a child. She would leave lipstick stains on my cream-coloured, Chinese silk kurtas as she 'kissed' me bye-bye, and my wife would . . . well you understand.

I told Atma, 'Tell them I don't like all this, it causes problems at home.' He conveyed my instructions to them. But subsequently Mala Sinha and Tanuja entered into a pact of mischief. One evening, while we were still at work, Tanuja came over to sit by my side. She felt the sleeve of my kurta. 'What is this, silk?' she asked. 'Yes,' I responded, wondering what she was up to. Without a warning, she pushed the sleeve of the kurta up my arm and bit my biceps hard. 'You don't want lipstick marks—take this home instead.' I had a lot of explaining to do when my wife saw the damage Tanuja's teeth had done.

Needless to say, I had my revenge. I literally took her to task on the sets, till she ran away crying. Mala Sinha too used to throw quite a few tantrums. I decided to play tough with her, and finally made her run to her room, in tears. Atma came up asking what had happened. I said, 'I've done my bit, made her cry—now you do yours, take your kerchief . . .'

They would come in late by hours, and we were on a shoestring budget; it tried my patience. But after the dressing-down she received, Mala Sinha was always on time. In fact, she became very polite and started calling me by a nickname she gave me: Jaaneman!

But for all my troubles I was credited only as the film's writer.

As it turned out, the film's credits mention Shahid Lateef as director. Abrar is not forthcoming about why he did not seek directorial credit. It could be because he did not believe in it, and was doing the job only to salvage the company. A failure at the box office, *Baharen Phir Bhi Aayengi* is today remembered primarily for being associated with Guru Dutt's death and its song, hauntingly rendered by Rafi, '*Aap ke haseen rukh pe aaj naya noor hai*'.

Atma Ram, who was eventually credited as controller of production of *Baharen*, directed *Shikar*, a suspenseful thriller, for Guru Dutt Films soon after. The film starred Dharmendra and Asha Parekh in the lead. Once again, Abrar stood by Atma and helped him scene by scene, literally taking over the reins. In the end, he was credited only for the dialogues. *Shikar* became a silver-jubilee hit and was nominated for four Filmfare Awards: Sanjeev Kumar for best supporting actor, Johnny Walker for best comedian, Asha Bhonsle for best female playback singer for that hit number '*Parde mein rahne do*', and P. Thakkersey for best sound recordist. Thakkersey was the lone winner. Atma Ram went on to produce and direct a few films in the early 1970s. Prominent among these were *Umang*, which made news for casting a whole crop of newcomers including Subhash Ghai, and *Yeh Gulistan Hamara*, starring Dev Anand.

Abrar never wielded the megaphone again. Over the years he proved his writing credentials with films like *Sunghursh* (1968), which had some memorable dialogues, and the Rishi Kapoor box-office hit *Laila Majnu* (1976). But nothing quite measured up to the heights he had scaled with Guru Dutt. To paraphrase an unforgettable Hollywood dialogue, after ten years with Guru Dutt, 'It is the pictures that got small'.

The Guru Dutt Filmography

As Dance Director

Hum Ek Hain (1946)
Director: P.L. Santoshi
Main cast: Dev Anand, Rehana

As Assistant Director

Lakharani (1945)
Director: Vishram Bedekar
Main cast: Durga Khote,
Monica Desai, Sapru. Guru
Dutt acted in it as well.

Mohan (1947)
Director: A.N. Banerji
Main cast: Dev Anand, Hemavati

Girl's School (1949)
Director: Amiya Chakravarty
Main cast: Geeta Bali, Sajjan,
Shashikala

Sangram (1950)
Director: Gyan Mukherjee
Main cast: Ashok Kumar,
Nalini Jaywant

As Director

Baazi (1951)
Producer: Navketan Films
Main cast: Dev Anand, Geeta
Bali, Kalpana Kartik, K.N. Singh

Jaal (1952)
Producer: Film Arts
Main cast: Dev Anand, Geeta
Bali, K.N. Singh

Sailaab (1956)
Main cast: Abhi Bhattacharya,
Geeta Bali, Ram Singh, Smriti
Biswas

As Producer, Actor, Director

Baaz (1953)
Producer: Haridarshan Gurudutt
Films (This film was
produced in partnership
between Geeta Bali's sister
and Guru Dutt)
Main cast: Guru Dutt, Geeta
Bali, K.N. Singh
Music Director: O.P. Nayyar
Editor: Y.G. Chavan
Cinematographer: V.K. Murthy

Aar Paar (1954)
Producer: Guru Dutt Films Pvt.
Ltd
Main cast: Guru Dutt, Shyama,
Shakila, Johnny Walker
Music Director: O.P. Nayyar
Lyricist: Majrooh Sultanpuri

Editor: Y.G. Chavan
Cinematographer: V.K. Murthy

Mr and Mrs '55 (1955)
Producer: Guru Dutt Films Pvt.
Ltd
Main cast: Guru Dutt, Madhubala,
Lalita Pawar, Johnny Walker
Music Director: O.P. Nayyar
Lyricist: Majrooh Sultanpuri
Editor: Y.G. Chavan
Cinematographer: V.K. Murthy

Pyaasa (1957)
Producer: Guru Dutt Films Pvt.
Ltd
Main cast: Guru Dutt, Mala Sinha,
Waheeda Rehman, Rehman,
Johnny Walker
Music Director: S.D. Burman
Lyricist: Sahir Ludhianvi
Editor: Y.G. Chavan
Cinematographer: V.K. Murthy

Kaagaz Ke Phool (1959)
Producer: Guru Dutt Films Pvt.
Ltd
Main cast: Guru Dutt, Waheeda
Rehman, Johnny Walker
Music Director: S.D. Burman
Lyricist: Kaifi Azmi
Editor: Y.G. Chavan
Cinematographer: V.K. Murthy

As Producer, Actor

Chaudhvin Ka Chand (1960)
Producer: Guru Dutt Films Pvt.
Ltd
Director: M. Sadiq
Main cast: Guru Dutt, Waheeda
Rehman, Rehman, Johnny
Walker

Music Director: Ravi
Lyricist: Shakeel Badayuni
Editor: Y.G. Chavan
Cinematographer: Nariman Irani

Sahib Bibi Aur Ghulam (1962)
Producer: Guru Dutt Films Pvt.
Ltd
Main cast: Guru Dutt, Meena
Kumari, Waheeda Rehman,
Rehman, Sapru
Director: Abrar Alvi
Music Director: Hemant Kumar
Lyricist: Shakeel Badayuni
Editor: Y.G. Chavan
Cinematographer: V.K. Murthy

As Producer

CID (1956)
Producer: Guru Dutt Films Pvt.
Ltd
Director: Raj Khosla
Main cast: Dev Anand, Shakila,
Johnny Walker and introducing
Waheeda Rehman
Music Director: O.P. Nayyar
Lyricist: Majrooh Sultanpuri
Editor: Y.G. Chavan
Cinematographer: V.K. Murthy,
Anwar

As Actor

12 O'Clock (1958)
Director: Pramod Chakravorty
Main cast: Guru Dutt,
Waheeda Rehman, Shashikala

Sautela Bhai (1962)
Director: Mahesh Kaul
Main cast: Guru Dutt, Pronoti
Ghosh

Bahurani (1963)
Director: T. Prakash Rao
Main cast: Guru Dutt, Mala Sinha, Feroz Khan

Bharosa (1963)
Director: K. Shankar
Main cast: Guru Dutt, Asha Parekh, Mehmood, Shubha Khote

Sanjh Aur Savera (1964)
Director: Hrishikesh Mukherjee
Main cast: Guru Dutt, Meena Kumari, Mehmood, Shubha Khote

Suhagan (1964)
Director: K.S. Gopalakrishnan
Main cast: Guru Dutt, Mala Sinha, Feroz Khan, Nasir Hussain

Incomplete Productions

Gauri (1957): This was to have launched wife Geeta Dutt as a singing star and was to be India's first-ever film in cinemascope.

Raaz (1959): Based on Wilkie Collins's *The Woman in White*, this was to have been music director R.D. Burman's maiden film.

Kaneez (1962): A fantasy based on *The Arabian Nights*, this was to have been Guru Dutt's first feature film in colour.

Baharen Phir Bhi Aayengi (1963–64): Guru Dutt died while this film was under production. It was subsequently completed by brother Atma Ram with Dharmendra in the lead and released in 1966.

Other Incomplete Films

Love and God (1963–64): Produced and directed by K. Asif, Guru Dutt was the leading man of this film. When he died, the role was taken over by Sanjeev Kumar. Both Asif and Sanjeev Kumar died before completing the film. Producer K.C. Bokadia completed it by using doubles and released it in 1986.

Picnic (1964): This film starring Guru Dutt and Sadhana was shelved.

Besides these, there were announcements of films to be made, for example, *Professor*, starring Kishore Kumar and Waheeda Rehman, and many ideas were contemplated upon but unfortunately never saw the light of day.

The Abrar Alvi Filmography

As Writer (Screenplay and/or Dialogue)

FOR GURU DUTT FILMS PVT. LTD

Aar Paar (1954)

Mr and Mrs '55 (1955)

Pyaasa (1957)

Kaagaz Ke Phool (1959)

Chaudhvin Ka Chand (1960)

Sahib Bibi Aur Ghulam (1962)

Baharen Phir Bhi Aayengi (1966)
Director: Shahid Lateef
Main cast: Dharmendra, Mala
  Sinha, Tanuja

Shikar (1968)
Director: Atma Ram
Main cast: Dharmendra, Asha
  Parekh, Sanjeev Kumar, Helen

OTHER BANNERS

Professor (1962)
Director: Lekh Tandon
Main cast: Shammi Kapoor,
  Kalpana, Lalita Pawar

Suraj (1966)
Director: T. Prakash Rao
Main cast: Vyjayanthimala,
  Rajendra Kumar, Ajit

Chhoti Si Mulaqat (1967)
Director: Alo Sircar
Main cast: Vyjayanthimala,
  Uttam Kumar, Rajendra
  Nath, Shashikala

Sunghursh (1968)
Director: H.S. Rawail
Main cast: Dilip Kumar,
  Vyjayanthimala, Sanjeev
  Kumar, Balraj Sahni, Jayant

Saathi (1968)
Director: C.V. Sridhar
Main cast: Vyjayanthimala,
  Rajendra Kumar, Simi Garewal

Manoranjan (1974)
Director: Shammi Kapoor
Main cast: Sanjeev Kumar, Zeenat
  Aman, Shammi Kapoor

Laila Majnu (1976)
Director: H.S. Rawail
Main cast: Rishi Kapoor,
  Ranjeeta, Danny Denzongpa

Bairaag (1976)
Director: Asit Sen
Main cast: Dilip Kumar, Saira
  Banu, Leena Chandavarkar,
  Prem Chopra

Sabse Bada Rupaiya (1976)
Director: S. Ramanathan

Main cast: Mehmood, Vinod
Mehra, Moushumi Chatterjee

Hamare Tumhare (1979)
Director: Umesh Mehra
Main cast: Sanjeev Kumar,
Rakhee, Amjad Khan

Biwi-O-Biwi (1981)
Director: Rahul Rawail
Main cast: Sanjeev Kumar,
Randhir Kapoor, Poonam
Dhillon, Yogeeta Bali

Khuda Kasam (1981)
Director: Lekh Tandon
Main cast: Vinod Khanna, Tina
Munim, Ajit, Pran

Patthar Dil (1985)
Director: Surendra Mohan
Main cast: Padmini Kolhapuri,
Danny Denzongpa, Kader Khan

Janam Janam (1988)
Director: Vijay Sadanah
Main cast: Rishi Kapoor, Vinita
Goel, Danny Denzongpa,
Amrish Puri

Kasam Suhag Ki (1989)
Director: Mohan Segal
Main cast: Dharmendra, Rekha,
Suresh Oberoi, Gulshan
Grover, Sadashiv Amrapurkar

Guddu (1995)
Director: Prem Lalwani
Main cast: Shah Rukh Khan,
Manisha Koirala, Deepti
Naval, Mukesh Khanna

As Actor

Mr and Mrs '55 (1955),
directed by Guru Dutt

CID (1956), directed by Raj
Khosla

12 O'Clock (1958), directed by
Pramod Chakravorty

Laila Majnu (1976), directed by
H.S. Rawail

As Director

Sahib Bibi Aur Ghulam (1962)